LIVING WITH
DEMENTIA

LIVING WITH DEMENTIA

◆

A LOVE STORY

ELAINE K. WINIK

iUniverse, Inc.
New York Lincoln Shanghai

LIVING WITH DEMENTIA
A LOVE STORY

iUniverse books may be ordered through booksellers or by contacting:

iUniverse
2021 Pine Lake Road, Suite 100
Lincoln, NE 68512
www.iuniverse.com
1-800-Authors (1-800-288-4677)

ISBN-13: 978-0-595-38373-3 (pbk)
ISBN-13: 978-0-595-82747-3 (ebk)
ISBN-10: 0-595-38373-4 (pbk)
ISBN-10: 0-595-82747-0 (ebk)

Printed in the United States of America

This book is dedicated to my family, all of whom have been so supportive, and to Linda Chow without whom I couldn't have managed. Above all I dedicate it to the love of my life, Norman, who in the face of all he has lost, has managed to remain kind, loving and appreciative.

Contents

PREFACE

Why I Wrote This Book

If you are looking for a scientific text on Dementia you are reading the wrong book. I am neither a neurologist nor a psychiatrist. My aim is simply to share this journey my husband and I have had to take and to show how we have managed to keep our dignity, our sense of humor and above all, our love for one another.

I know how lucky I am that I have had a wonderful person to help me with Norm and to give me some free time. Linda, his caregiver loves him and he feels the same way about her. That is a great comfort, but everyone who is involved in caring for a beloved person with dementia will feel the emotional impact. This pertains to all of us whether or not there is someone to share the load.

My special wish is that this book may help other caregivers. What you will have to adjust to will not be easy but it need not be soul destroying.

I have kept a diary, since the beginning of Norm's illness, and I have included segments of it in hope that the reader will get a true feeling of what life can be like living with a loved one who is suffering from dementia. There have been times when Norm seemed to have slipped down a notch and I have looked back at the diary and discovered that what I thought of as a further loss was a behavior that had manifested itself before. Is that a comfort to me? I'm not sure, but anything that isn't a sign of further decays, I regard as a plus.

THE NIGHT IS FULL OF FEAR 1994

The night is full of fear
He who was strong is weak and needy
"I'm frightened," he says
And I reach out
I want to share my strength
But do I have enough?
Will my good health be an affront or a consolation?
My face aches from smiling

"You'll be fine darling," I say
Wondering if he believes me
My thoughts turn dark
Is this to be the shape of my future?
Only children and fools think they are immortal
Time robs us all
No one is immune to its ravages
"Darling," he says again, "I'm frightened
I smile brightly
"You'll be fine," I say

At the onset of my husband Norman's dementia he was seventy-three, and I was seventy-two, but we both felt young and healthy. Since then it has been over ten years on a roller coaster, good days and bad, times of hope and times of despair. Having lived with his dementia all these years, my aim is to try to give some moral support to others who are in this position and who sometimes feel as though they are alone in the world.

When Norm's dementia was first diagnosed I thought that my life had come to an end. But I soon learned that while brain cells may die, love is harder to kill.

I have kept a diary so that I could pour my heart out to it. Instead of screaming or crying, I write. It always makes me feel a little better. As time passed I seem to have written less often, not because I've gotten lazy but because with dementia so many things happen over and over. I would notice a "new" symptom, read my diary and discover that the same thing had happened two or three months earlier.

At the beginning of Norm's dementia everyone counseled me to, "Find some time for yourself. The caregiver often dies before the patient." I can't tell you how I resented this advice. I believed that if and when Norman needed me, I had to be there. Well, they were right and I was wrong.. t took me a long time to understand that finding time and space for oneself is not selfish, it is the only way to keep the ability to be patient with the person who needs your patience, love and support, as never before. I have come to believe that the person with dementia often retains a sense of what has been lost and desperately needs reassurance. You must give yourself some breathing room so you can provide that reassurance.

Each case is as different as the person who is affected and each caregiver must ultimately discover what works best for him or her. But there are certain things which always pertain in this situation, anyone suffering from dementia needs to feel loved and accepted. It won't be easy and there will be times when you don't know whether you will able to cope. But then something of the person you used to know will shine through. The joy you feel when he remembers the lyrics of an old song and begins to sing in the strong voice you never thought you would hear again, or when you see a smile when you share something funny and he gets the joke. These are among a hundred little things which give you the courage to go on.

CHAPTER ONE

Our marriage is a second one for both of us. Norm's first wife had died. He had two adult daughters, one of whom was already married. He was a Yale graduate and had been a captain in the Marine Air Corps in world War II, where he spent almost two years as a dive-bomber pilot in the south Pacific. Later in civilian life he became the owner of several tennis clubs and camps.

As for me I was divorced with a son and two daughters. When we met I was the national chairwoman of the United Jewish Appeal, a full time volunteer. We had known one another for years, although not well. I knew his wife much better than I knew him.

Actually we had double-dated at a Yale prom when I was sixteen and he was seventeen. I didn't pay much attention to him (I had my own date) but I thought his date was beautiful, and so sophisticated, which I was not. She was the woman he married. We later moved into the same area and we would meet now and again at parties given by mutual friends.

Strange to think of how often fate seemed to bring us together. I remember walking up Fifth Avenue with my first husband. It was during World War Two. Burt was a Boatswains Mate first class in the Navy and was wearing his sailor suit. I am and have always been, nearsighted and as we approached Fifty Seventh-Street I turned to Burt and said, "Will you look at the gorgeous doorman Tiffany has." He looked and said, "That's not a doorman. That's Norman Winik in his Marine Corps uniform."

So how did we get together after all those years? I was about to be divorced from my husband. My private life was a mess but my career was going beautifully. As the national chair of the Women's Division of the United Jewish Appeal, I traveled all over the world to wherever a Jewish community was in danger, or wherever there were funds to be raised. I was in Rumania while Ceausescu was in power, I visited Morocco, and went into Iran while it was ruled by the Shah. I met trainloads of Russian immigrants at the Vienna railroad station, I called Golda Meir a friend and I had tea in the kitchen of Ben Gurion and his wife Paula. I stood at the Suez Canal five days after The Six Days War was over. I climbed the Golan Heights before all the mines and animal carcasses had been removed.

I had known of Carolyn Winik's illness and I certainly would have gone to her funeral but I was in Israel when she died. On my return I wrote Norm a condolence letter. A few days later I got an answer, "I received hundreds of letters", he wrote, "I've saved your letter because you said something very meaningful to me. There is an important matter I would like to discuss with you but I know how busy you are. Would you call me at your earliest opportunity?"

I called him on a Monday and said I could see him a week from Thursday, because I knew that the man I was going out with was busy that night.

"Can we have dinner? he asked.

I said I would be delighted.

Thursday evening at seven the door bell rang and I answered it. I kissed Norm hello in the way one kisses an old friend, and asked him to come in for a drink. As we went in I started to talk about Carolyn. He began to cry. "No one lets me talk about her," he said. "But isn't she what you want to talk about?" I asked. We talked and talked and had a martini…maybe two…and then went out for dinner. There we talked some more. It seemed perfectly normal to me to be speaking to a comparative stranger about intimate feelings on the loss of a loved one. It never occurred to me that this was something Norm didn't do. I soon learned that Norm is a very private person, who doesn't confide in strangers and I still can't believe how open he was with me, that openness became an important part of our relationship.

Finally I asked him what the important matter was that he had to talk to me about. Norm said his rabbi had asked if there wasn't anyone in the congregation who had the courage to move to Israel and help build the country with his own hands. "The idea stayed in my mind," he said," And I was just going to call the rabbi and discuss it with him when I got your letter." He continued, "I thought to myself, she knows more about Israel than the rabbi. I'll ask her."

I looked at him and asked, "Do you want an honest answer?

He said he did.

"Israel is a wonderful country, but not an easy place to live" I said, "You are in a million pieces now. Pull yourself together, get yourself whole and then move to Israel."

He pulled himself together. Five months later we were married and he changed his mind about moving anywhere…except into my house.

We were both in our early fifties when we married and all of our children were grown and living their own lives. You have heard people speak about "the perfect marriage," ours was just that. For our honeymoon we drove to every part of Israel, with a short, mistaken detour into Syria. Instead of being frightened, as we should have been, we just laughed. Nothing could threaten us as long as we were together. My life's work had been the helping to build the Jewish state. Watching Norm fall in love with Israel was magical for me.

What a change of life I had elected to make. One Friday I was in Washington D.C. talking to my senator about foreign aid and on Sunday I was the camp mother to one hundred and two young tennis players, ranging in age from nine to fourteen. While Norm ran the camp I was responsible for the homesick kids and for their camp bank accounts. I loved the kids but I'm a mathematical illiterate. Numbers like $.50 $1.00 I could handle but $1.43 deducted for shampoo could throw me....and there were lots of $1.43s. Shampoo seemed to have been a popular item.

Every summer we would leave our beautiful home on Long Island Sound and move into a small apartment on the campus of a boarding school. Believe me, the accommodations were less than palatial...but we had fun. We did room inspections and cookouts. We handed out awards and settled fights...and after all the kids were asleep we would each take a glass of vodka and sit and laugh as we shared the day's activities.

Norman's business during the rest of the year was not very time consuming and as we were each financially independent we were able to travel a great deal. I'll never forget the day that Norman came running in from the terrace shouting, "Darling, read this article in the Travel Section of the Times. It sounds great." I did, and a few weeks later we were on a trek in the Himalayas. We spent ten magical days, waking up to the sight of Everest towering above us. We slept in a tent and washed in a tin bowl. With our Sherpa guides at our side we hiked as much as fifteen miles a day. It was one of the most wonderful experiences either of us had ever had.

CHAPTER TWO

As I shared Norm's love of running a tennis camp, he was anxious to learn more about my work. In 1985, when I was asked to lead a group of people to the Soviet Union to see refusniks, (Jews who had been fired from their jobs for wanting to leave the country but had been denied exit permits) he came along as did my two daughters. There were about thirty of us in all and we broke up into smaller groups so as to be less visible to the authorities. Two groups flew into Moscow and one into Leningrad now Saint Petersburg. Our group landed in Leningrad,

The first four people went through immigration without a hitch. This was going to be easy, I thought. Easy? The oh-so-charming Soviet police separated Norman, my daughters and me. For about three hours they kept Norman in one room, each of my daughters in another and me in the fourth. There was certainly no physical torture but the constant questioning was scary. Then each of us was accused of being a" Zionist spy" and told that we might as well confess since the others had.

Finally we were each given a document written in Russian and told to sign it. The State Department had told us in a briefing that if this should happen, we were to sign and then write under it, "I don't read Russian and I don't know what I have signed." We did as we had been told. Soon after, our tormentors decided that we could join our waiting friends and go into the city.

Of course our transportation to Leningrad had long since gone so we had to sit and wait until more taxis arrived. While we waited we told our friends what had happened to us. Then two of the goons came back into the waiting room. They told the others that they were welcome in the Soviet Union, but that Norm, my daughters and I were not fit for that privilege. We were to come to another part of the airport and wait until morning when a plane would take us back to New York.

Norm, who is slow to anger, turned, pointed his finger almost in one man's eye and said, "Nyet! Do you know what nyet means? Then he added, "You want a plane to take us home? You bring it here. We are not moving." Then he whispered to me, "Break out the vodka." I took out a bottle of vodka. My daughter Margot had several cans of tomato juice and my other daughter Penny had crackers. (We had been advised to bring these things...except for the vodka.) We sat down on the floor and had a cocktail party.

The Russians looked at us as if we were crazy. Then they left, apparently to ask their superior what to do. Ten minutes later they came back. "Go ahead to Leningrad," they said. That was the beginning of our trip. Without Norm's nerve I don't think they would have let us in.

CHAPTER THREE

Neither Norm nor I who had ever really looked at a bird before became avid bird-watchers. Binoculars in hand we went down the Amazon gasping at the brightly colored macaws, the pre historic quetzals and listening to the wonderful songs of the nun birds. In Kenya we learned that the African version of the lowly starling had morphed into something magnificent and multi-colored, there it was called supreme starling and it certainly was supreme.

We went into inlets of the Amazon in rubber rafts and "talked" to the natives. Smiles and pictures of grandchildren can go far in establishing communications. Norm had a trick that never failed to mesmerize the children. He would squat down and pretend that he was taking off his left thumb as the kids gathered around, laughing, gasping and trying to do it themselves. It opened doors for us as these children ran home to tell their parents to come and see the "magic." The parents were usually as amazed as the children, and often invited us back to their homes. Most of these homes were huts with bare floors and either thatch or tin roofs, but the friendliness and hospitality more than compensated for the surroundings.

Snorkeling became one of our favorite pastimes and we saw the brightly colored fish and coral in Sharm-el-Sheik, the Great Barrier Reef and many other places. We swam with barracudas and sting rays. We were told that at low tide in the Amazon piranhas weren't dangerous, so we swam with those too. Norm was a lot more daring than I was, but as time went on I seemed to borrow some of his courage.

We marveled at the huge statues on Easter Island, and watched Polar Bears above the Arctic Circle. We drove to the Grand Canyon in a camper, hiked to the bottom and up again. We slept in sleeping bags in the Sinai, went on a safari in Kenya and Tanzania, and climbed up to Macchu Picchu. One of our most exciting trips was paddling down the Sepik River in New Guinea. Until we ran out of strength we took each grandchild on a tenth birthday trip, one down the rapids of the Colorado, one rafting on the Yukon, and another snorkeling in Bonaire. We drove to the Maritime Provinces of Canada with another and took the youngest to a dude ranch in Montana. We always picked a place where we could all relax and not worry about dressing up. The children loved their trips and so did we. Sadly we ran out of energy before we ran out of grandchildren and the three youngest ones never did get their trips.

But this is not a travel book and of course we didn't spend our whole time traveling. The foregoing is just to give you a picture of two people relishing the world and one another. Norm had a business to run and I was busy with my full-time volunteer work. In his spare time Norm cultivated a huge vegetable garden while I grew flowers in abundance. Our house was and is always full of flowers, I loved picking and arranging them, and still do. In the late summer Norm would bring in armloads of eggplants, zucchinis, cucumbers and even once in a while (if we got there before the raccoons) an ear or two of corn. A mediocre cook at best, I learned to make a stunning variety of cold soups which friends and family enjoyed sharing. Norm, on the other hand, became a really good cook. He made wonderful stir-fried dishes, beer batter shrimp and vegetables and he even pickled his own cucumbers.

I have always been an early riser, but after we were married I would open my eyes at six thirty in the morning to find Norm gone. He was out on his two mile run. For a while I tried to join him but it was more than I could manage. Even togetherness has to have its limits. Still we couldn't seem to get enough of being together and even the most ordinary things became exciting when they were shared.

My responsibilities at the United Jewish Appeal required a certain amount of travel. Not only did I have to lead groups to Israel but I also had to travel around the country making fund raising speeches. Norm always said that he was a very good sport about it. Was he? I'm not sure, but for my birthday he gave me a gold bracelet engraved with the letters IDTA. He explained that when the UJA asked me to go out of town I was to look at the bracelet and say, I Did That Already....IDTA.

I tried it for a couple of months and then told Norm that if he wanted me to stay home he should stay home with me. I couldn't stand doing nothing. We agreed that I should continue my work, but on a reduced schedule. Who knew that soon I would need all my time for him?

We read the same books and then discussed what we had read. We shared the New York Times crossword puzzle. Concerts and theater were an integral part of our lives. Just being together was our greatest pleasure. We were living a wonderful dream when the whole world began to change.

CHAPTER FOUR

How could I not have noticed the changes that were taking place in Norman? It doesn't seem possible but they were so gradual that it was easy to chalk them up to mood swings, which he never had and still doesn't have, or to depression, or even to me. I must be getting impatient, I thought. After all everyone gets forgetful as they age, why should I be upset if Norm repeats himself? Could I have been so blind? Apparently I was.

Looking through my files the other day I found the following story. I had put it on paper and then put it out of my mind. It was not a pleasant memory.

My oldest sister, Mickey, had moved to senior housing in Washington D.C. Her granddaughter who lived in the Washington area persuaded her to move there so that she could visit her every day. To her credit, she did.

Norm and I decided to visit Mickey who had not been well. We drove to LaGuardia airport and got on the shuttle plane. I may have rushed Norm a little bit because I hate sitting in the back of the plane and there are no reserved seats on the shuttle. As it worked out we were closer to the back than to the front but at least we were seated next to one another.

We settled into our seats and I looked at Norman. "Darling," I said, "you look pale. Are you all right?"

"I'm a little dizzy," he said, "But it will pass." Maybe it would, I thought, but he was dead white and his hands were shaking.

"Would you like a glass of water?" I asked.

"Please."

I got him a glass of water which he gulped down. "You know darling," I said," we can go to see Mickey another day. And if you really don't feel well it's better to get off right now than to make the plane turn around enroute to Washington.

"I'm all right," he insisted

A man sitting behind us who apparently did not want to be late getting to Washington, must have rung the bell for the flight attendant, and before we knew it Norm was being carried off the plane on a stretcher, with me following right behind.

When we got to the ambulance I told the paramedics that our car was in the parking lot. "Just take us there," I said, "and I'll take him to our doctor."

"You don't understand lady," one of them said, "We have to take him to the nearest hospital."

A word of warning, don't ever get sick at La Guardia because the nearest hospital was designed by Charles Dickens and the staff were all modeled on a combination of Ebenezer Scrooge and that character who wouldn't give Oliver Twist any more porridge.

As we went into the emergency room entrance I saw several men bleeding copiously from gashes on their faces. I saw people reeling either from drugs or alcohol. The floor was less than spotless and the air was full of screams and moans.

As Norm was wheeled into the emergency room I started to follow him. "No lady," I was told, "You can't go in there."

"Oh yes I can." I said with more bravado then I felt. I followed him and no one else said anything.

After about twenty minutes a doctor appeared, took one look and said, "We will have to admit him. He has had a heart attack."

"You can't admit him;" I said. "I don't believe he has had a heart attack and besides, I'm going to call our own doctor." I did just that and our doctor, who happens to be a cardiologist, told me to put Norm in an ambulance and take him to United Hospital where he could look after him.

I conveyed this to the doctor and his answer was quick and concise. "I will not discharge him. So if you take him out it's on your head and besides that, without a discharge you will have to pay for the ambulance yourself. The insurance won't cover it"

By this time the color had returned to Norm's face. He kept saying to me, "Get me out of this hell hole. I can't stand all the screaming."

The ambulance came in about twenty minutes and we got in and started the half hour or so drive to Port Chester. Norm was cheerful and talkative the whole ride. As for me, I started breathing again. When we got to the hospital Norm was admitted. He had an Electro-cardiogram which the doctor in Flushing, (or wherever it was,) had neglected to do. His heart was fine. The doctor's diagnosis, "As close as I can figure, he has had a panic attack." That should have set off alarm bells in my head. I had never seen Norm panic and we had been in more than one scary situation.

"Let him stay overnight,'" the doctor added, "just so I can keep an eye on him. But I'm sure he'll be fine."

Next morning I drove him home, and the following day he was back at work.

My sister died that week, I had missed the chance for a last visit. The insurance company reimbursed four hundred of the six hundred and fifty dollars the ambulance cost. My daughter drove me to LaGuardia where I got my car, and we resumed, I thought, our normal life. In retrospect I must have known something was wrong because soon after I started to keep a diary.

CHAPTER FIVE

My First Diary Entry
May 10, 1996

This will not be easy but I feel that I must keep a record of the strange and terrifying things that are happening to Norman and me. There is nothing worse than watching the person who is closest to you disintegrate before your eyes. At first the changes were so slight as to be almost imperceptible and I was able to deny to myself that anything was wrong. But finally I had to face the fact that Norman, the strong take-charge person I had married was gone. He no longer seemed able to make a decision. Now it was all left to me...O.K., I decided, that could be handled.

The next thing I noticed were the memory lapses. "Darling," he would say, "I must call the office."

"Sweetheart, you just hung up."

"Oh, did I?" Five minutes later the same thing...and again five minutes after that. He can't help it I thought, don't get upset, and just make a diagram for him. I took a piece of construction paper and wrote "CALL THE OFFICE, opposite that I wrote CHECK HERE.." It worked for a little while Then he lost the paper and the interest. All he really wanted to do was sleep.

Yesterday there was a frightening manifestation of this illness. Norm woke from a nap and asked in a shaky voice, "What's wrong with me? I never used to be like this."

"Sweetheart," I said "as we get older there will be good days and bad...but at least we're together." That seemed to comfort him.

DIARY May 15, 1996

Darling," Norman said, "can you come with me to the bank? I don't remember how to use the ATM machine." Of course I went. Once we got there he handed me his ATM card and said, "You do it, darling, I'm feeling a little confused today."

Thinking I had to take his mind off his problems, I bought tickets to the Satur-day matinee of a Broadway show called RENT. He said he was anxious to go. By the end of the first act he was trembling, "It's too noisy for me," he said. And in truth the show was miked almost to the point of pain. We left. I've seen enough shows so that one act more or less won't kill me. As we walked to the parking lot he said, "I'm such a jerk. I don't know how you put up with me." Yet with each step he seemed to become calmer.

I must find a way to keep him stimulated, I told myself, but not to the point of frightening him.

DIARY May 18, 1996

He woke this morning and asked for a tranquilizer, "I'm so jumpy," he said, "Something awful is happening. How can a mind as sharp as mine just disap-pear?"

He thought a minute and then asked, "Am I losing my mind?"

"No, darling," I said, "You are losing your memory." Strangely that seemed to comfort him.

That was the onset of his dementia and my life on a roller coaster. I call it that because one day he seems his old self and I rejoice, the next day he remembers nothing and I'm in the depths of despair. However over the years I have learned not to react to every change, for with dementia nothing seems to be permanent.

CHAPTER SIX

Searching for a Doctor Who Could Help

At the very beginning of my husband's illness I was convinced that this very cheerful and optimistic man had somehow become depressive. We went to a psychiatrist who had been recommended to us. He agreed that Norman was in a depression and prescribed a mood elevator. It did no good. Norm became more and more forgetful and lethargic and his mood didn't improve. I was frightened. I knew there was something wrong and I had to get to the bottom of it. So began our time of doctor shopping.

We went to a very prestigious institute for Aging and Dementia where they gave my husband every test one could imagine and then a few more. He was terribly nervous and kept asking, "Why are we here?" I assured him that he was being tested to see what was bothering him. He accepted that with, "As long as you don't leave me I know I'll be all right." While he was being tested I went to the head of the department and said," If it is Alzheimer's, please don't tell him. Tell me so I can break it to him gently." The doctor said that would not be a problem, and that if I felt it was important for me to tell him the results, they would certainly honor my wishes.

A few weeks later after all the tests were done we were asked to come to a meeting. I can still see the large conference room, overlooking the East River in New York City.

"What a beautiful view, "I said to Norm, trying to behave as if this were an ordinary conference on an ordinary day. But it wasn't and we both knew it. In the center of the room was a long narrow table, around which sat an assortment of psychiatrists, psychologists, social workers and geriatricians. The psychiatrist at the head of the table took out a big red folder and thumbed through the pages. As he did he kept saying, "Negative, negative, negative" My spirits began to rise. Then he turned to my husband and said, "Mr. Winik, we have ruled out a number of things, among them stroke and brain tumor" (He mentioned a few other possible causes but I was beginning to feel so optimistic that my mind must have drifted.),

He continued, looking intently at Norman, "We have come to the conclusion that you are in the early stages of late-onset Alzheimer's."

I saw a look of panic cross Norm's face. I glared at the doctor. What had happened to the promise he had given me? I wanted to touch Norm, to hold him in my arms and say that the doctor was wrong, but this was a medical conference and all I could do was hold his hand as tightly as possible. We sat there until the doctors told us basically that there was little they could suggest but that since this was a research institute and they wanted us to come back for tests every few months. They were obviously more interested in the disease than in the patient. I can't blame them, that's what they were there for, but my interest was the patient.

"You know, Mr. Winik," the doctor continued, as if offering consolation, "at your age Alzheimer's disease moves very slowly. The life span of the average American male is seventy-four years so you could die of eight other things before this gets too bad."

At Norm's age! Seventy-four seemed so old to this forty year old doctor, but not to us. Norm was seventy-three at the time. But he was not a statistic. He was a wonderful human being and everything to me.

"What are we going to do, darling?" Norm asked. "Am I going to lose my mind?"

"You are not going to lose your mind," I told him, trying to sound both positive and optimistic. "What we are going to do is find another doctor." And so we did.

We were shown into the office of Dr. Leslie Libow at Mount Sinai Hospital. He had been highly recommended as a highly skilled geriatrician. A tall, good looking man he immediately put us both at ease.

"I don't believe Norman has Alzheimer's" I told him, knowing how doctors hate patients who diagnose but he took it with good humor and thank heavens he never asked me where I got my medical degree.

"I agree" he said. "It doesn't appear to be Alzheimer's. He certainly does not behave the way a person with Alzheimer's does. He seems so focused. Let's try a few more tests. I would like him to have a PET scan. Do you know what that is?"

I didn't and so he explained to me in layman's language that just as a CAT scan gives the picture of the structure of the brain, (in this case) the PET scan gives a picture of the chemical activity. "It can't possibly hurt Norman," he assured me "and it might help us get a positive diagnosis of his problem". Of course I agreed that Norm should have the PET scan. I remember the test involved injecting glucose into Norm's arm. I watched Norm sitting at a desk where he was given mathematical problems to solve. While this was taking place some kind of camera took hundreds of pictures per minute of his brain. When the test was over the doctor showed me whole areas of the brain that were dark and explained that not enough blood was getting through.

Still the doctor did more and more tests, including another M.R.I., to make sure of his diagnosis. Finally I was told that Norm had a circulatory dementia. The word DEMENTIA terrified me. There was something derogatory about it. I remember as a child a very retarded classmate being called "demented". Even she understood what an insult the word was. Still like almost everything else I have come to accept it. Now how was I to handle it? How could I help us to live with it?

Since that time many new drugs have been discovered, including Aricept, Remynyl and Namenda, none of which, sadly, provides a cure, but can sometimes slow down the deterioration. Norman has tried them all. I tell people that if someone suggested a cure could be achieved by building a fire in the middle of the living room and dancing around it, I would give it a try. There doesn't seem to be anything to lose.

CHAPTER SEVEN

Diary October 23, 1996

"I got into my car, closed the windows and screamed. I imagine anyone seeing me must have thought that I was totally insane. The truth is that I was preserving my sanity, not losing it. Venting is absolutely vital when one is in this situation. I was venting to myself and not to Norman. The person with whom I had always shared everything was now the person with whom I could not share this.

Of course you can't scream all the time, so what else can you do? Some physical exercise can be a big help. Do anything that gets the blood flowing, a long walk, a run if you have the energy, perhaps a workout or a swim at the local Y. When your body works hard your spirit can take a much-needed rest. What will my loved one do when I'm looking after myself? That's the question I used to ask. I finally learned the answer. As long as that person is secure, in a group, with a family member or a friend, try not to think about it. I never promised it would be easy, but I do promise you that you will be a better care-giver if you have made a little space for yourself.

I know that many people feel that a dementia or Alzheimer's patient should be told the truth about his or her condition. I think it depends on the patient. I felt strongly that Norm would be better off not knowing. If he had asked a direct question I think I would have answered it. Did I do the right thing? How can anyone ever know? All I did was obey my instincts and in this kind of situation instincts are sometimes more reliable than science

CHAPTER EIGHT

My Self-Education

I had to learn more about this frightening disease. Back in 1995 when Norm first showed signs of dementia there was much less information about it than there is now. Still there were books and articles to be found and I read everything I could find on the subject. I remember how shaky I was when I finished The Thirty Six hour Day. Luckily we have never gotten to the stage described in that book.

We' re all so proud of modern medicine and how we have conquered diseases like Polio, Smallpox and TB, and well we should be. But there is a cost to this progress. Today we are living so long that a huge percentage of people over eighty, and there are more and more of us every day, will likely spend the last years of our lives suffering from dementia or Alzheimer's disease. According to a study published in the Archives of Neurology, dementia affects one in twenty people over the age of sixty five and one in five over the age of eighty. I have also read that the cost of care for people in this condition in the US alone is over one billion dollars a year. Sadly Medicare doesn't cover the cost and few people have the necessary insurance. One can find statistics galore but my aim here is to talk about the terrible emotional costs to the families of those many sufferers.

I knew I had to find a way to help my husband and to keep both of us from giving in to despair.

Here are some of the goals I have set for myself;

1. Find humor wherever possible.

2. Simplify ordinary tasks for him, such as laying out his clothes, putting the toothpaste on his toothbrush and so on (then watch while he performs the tasks of dressing or teeth-brushing, or they might not be done properly.....or at all)

3. Avoid situations which would frighten or confuse him, such as large noisy parties.

4. See to it that both of us get plenty of exercise.

5. Avoid tension wherever possible

6. Remember not to quibble over the small stuff.

7. Establish a routine. Those suffering from this illness are much happier when there are certain routines that can be counted on.

I didn't always accomplish these goals, but I tried, and I am still trying.

In one respect I have had good training in care giving. For as long as I can remember my father was a sick man. He had a pituitary disease called acromegaly. It is a rare and still, these many years later, an incurable disease affecting all the extremities of the body. If acromegaly strikes in childhood the victim can grow to be ten feet tall, but if it doesn't appear until maturity then the hands, feet, jaw and rib cage all become distorted. My father didn't look like other kids' fathers and he was always in pain, yet all my childhood I watched my mother care for him with great love. That love kept him alive for much longer than any of his doctors had predicted. My mother never acted as if she were sacrificing herself, I'm sure she never thought she was. I'm grateful to my mother for many things, but for nothing more than setting this example.

Mother must have found comfort in her own way. My problem is that when I am tense and worried, I have a tendency to overeat. I wish I were one of those people who lose their appetites when they are unhappy. At least they keep their waistlines. Mine is gone for good I'm afraid. I know that in the scheme of things that's a small problem, but vanity never seems to go away.

CHAPTER NINE

DIARY APRIL 29, 1997

One of the most difficult adjustments I had was the need to make life-changing decisions on my own, decisions Norm and I would have shared. But now there was no choice. The cold weather was too hard on Norman so I decided that we should try a winter in Florida to see if life down there would be easier for us. After a year or two of renting an apartment there I realized that this was indeed a better place for us and I bought a lovely two bedroom apartment. We are near the ocean and there is a heated swimming pool in which we both swim every day. Many of our friends live in the area...which is a blessing. It's hard to make new friends when one of us is suffering from dementia. Not only are strangers frightened by the very mention of dementia, but Norm doesn't take to strangers.

At the same time I faced the fact that our beautiful home in Rye, New York was too expensive to maintain just for summer use, We both loved it. It wasn't a big house but it overlooked Long Island Sound and we had spent many happy years there. I knew that this was no time to get sentimental over things. I sold it and we moved to a much smaller house in Rye Brook. It has no view but neither does it have any steps...a trade we had to make.

Poor Norm didn't like giving up the house and still asks me why we had to do it. My answer is always the same," Because we couldn't afford it anymore." Sometimes he accepts this and sometimes he tells me that we could have gotten a mortgage. But as time passes he speaks of it less and less.

DIARY April 30, 1997

Dr. Libow called this morning and reiterated that he felt strongly that Norm did not have Alzheimer's. He said that Norm has a form of dementia caused by arteriosclerosis. He seemed to feel that was good news.... I'm not sure it makes a hell of a lot of difference. As I understand it, it might mean a slower rate of deterioration and less personality change...but I'm not sure. I'm going to call him today and see if he can clarify it for me. One thing I do know is that there doesn't seem to be any treatment for it. My latest worry is that all Norm wants to do is to sleep all the time.

DIARY May, 16, 1997

Friday Shimon Peres, an old friend who is now the foreign minister of Israel, was in town and I was very anxious to see him. I suggested that Norm could play bridge while I went to the city. "Oh, no," he said, "I want to see him." Of course it wasn't a matter of seeing Shimon but of being with me. We both went and while Norm was a little shaky he basically made it through. We stopped on the way home and bought some plants, both for his garden and for mine, but so far I haven't gotten him to plant anything. He turned to me and asked, "I haven't had a vegetable garden in years, have I?" That threw me, since he has had one every year since we've been married.

DIARY June 2, 1997

I am convinced that he is bored and feeling completely useless. Yesterday he insisted on driving to his tennis club, "Just to let them know I'm still here and to see what's going on," he said. No sooner had he gotten there then he called.... I had asked him to, and asked, "What do you want me to do here?" It's always "What do you want me to do?" or "What do want me to wear?" All initiative has gone. He knows it and says, "I feel so unsure of myself." This from a man who was always so self-assured...

I'll never forget the day when I got a call from Kit Byron who had bought the tennis club from Norman. I knew it would come but that didn't make it any easier. Kit wants Norm's office for himself. After all, he is now running the tennis club and besides that Norm hardly comes in any more. Kit wanted to tell me so that I could break it to Norm, but I insisted that he tell the two of us together. It wasn't easy for him and it certainly wasn't for us. We both cried. Not while Kit was around and Norm kept repeating, "I built this place. I built this place." One of the worst aspects of the whole thing is that he remembers there is something wrong and that it is connected with his office, but he can't recall the details, and keeps asking me what happened so I have to explain it to him over and over.

It is now eight years later he has not gone back to the tennis club. We drive by it often and I ask if he would like to go in and see it. His answer is always "no." He seems to know that it would be painful for him to be confronted with someone else in charge of what used to be his domain.

I must admit that I can understand his feelings, I never go back to look at our beautiful home on the water. What is past is past. One must learn to close doors.

DIARY September 17, 1997
I search for things for him to do, things which will interest but not overtax him. Yesterday after his post swimming nap, we took a walk in the nature conservancy and saw two wild turkeys and a muskrat. He was so interested that for a while he forgot to be tired and we must have walked at least a mile. That was a kind of a triumph. Of course the minute we got home he fell into bed, but he perked up for dinner and though I did much of the talking...mainly to cover for his silences...he did seem engaged.

DIARY November 23, 1997
My big mistake was in somehow thinking that once we got to Florida Norm would be Norm again. Of course I knew he wouldn't, but hope dies hard. I have seen steady deterioration, as much physical as mental. As a matter of fact the thing I notice most besides his very shaky hands is a sort of detachment of personality. He will sit by himself, not reading or even looking at TV. He loves to drive with me to do errands and then wants to sit in the car while I do them....without the radio on...just sitting, quietly, usually with the seat pushed all the way back and his eyes closed. Luckily he has never wandered so I feel it's safe to leave him in the car for just a few minutes.

DIARY November 26, 1997
Yesterday my good friend Natalie asked me if I was nervous about him falling and I said, "No, he is steady on his feet." Lesson number God knows what

about this illness, ever make a definitive statement about anything. Last night on our way to dinner at my niece and nephew's house he got out of the elevator, walked in the wrong direction and bumped into the wall! I straightened him out with some joke about his being too preoccupied to look where he was going and then a minute later he did it again. I guess I'll have to watch him more closely. I also think it's time to get him a cane.

DIARY December 16, 1997

I wake up every morning between five and six, worried and jumpy. It takes me a little while to figure things out I guess. This morning it came to me that living with insecurity, not knowing how he'll be from one hour to the next can be very unsettling. That should be basic I know, but I've been so busy thinking about him that I haven't given a great deal of thought to myself. I wonder how much he really comprehends about his condition. I hope not too much.

DIARY January 5, 1998

This week Norm had come home from his bridge game completely discouraged. So I was especially happy to get a call from his old friend Charlie.

"How did Norm feel he did at the game?" Charlie asked.

I told him Norm had told me that he had played very badly. Charlie said that Norm had not played badly at all but that he had arrived tense and after making the kind of mistake they all make now and again he said he had to go home. We both agreed that Norm has lost his confidence. Then Charlie said if it were a matter of his being afraid to absorb the losses the "boys" would divide them up. I was very touched but said that it wasn't the money and that the "boys" were entitled to their winnings for having him in the game.

"Oh no," he said, "It's not like that. He can hold his own and we want him here.

I could have jumped through the phone and kissed him. Maybe this week he would take half a valium and let me drive him over. Or maybe the valium would dull him…we go to see Dr. Libow today and I'll ask him.

DIARY MARCH 19, 1998

Norm seems to have absorbed the message I was trying to send, which is that he doesn't have to be a "macho man", and that he can admit when he is tired and doesn't like to drive and that I can take over. The truth is that I loved it when he drove, but I'm getting used to doing the driving and even getting better at it. He says that I'm a good driver. But then, he says everything I do is good.

DIARY May 5, 1998

Again I haven't written because of some technical trouble with the computer. But here I go.

Wednesday we did go to see Dr. Libow He spent quite a bit of time with us, after which he assured us that he was convinced that it was not Alzheimer's, but rather a form of dementia. He is always kind and honest with us, but I wanted more than kindness, I wanted a cure and we both know that a cure doesn't exist...one day it will...but not in our lifetime.

snorkeling in Bonnaire

Norm relaxing

train in Alaska

Riding an Elephant looking for tigers in Nepal

Hanging out the wash at 10,000 feet, Nepal

Getting ready for the trek in Nepal

Taking it easy on island of Jost Van Dyk

One of the wonderful statues on Easter Island

The tiny bathtub in Paris

With our grandchildren on the Endless Summer, West Indies

CHAPTER TEN

Second Marriages

Many of us will have to deal with being part of reconstituted families. When my husband was first diagnosed with dementia I found his daughters very critical of me and, to be honest, very much concerned over the financial ramifications of his illness. I was now responsible for the fiscal part of our lives, (a job I would gladly have given up), and they probably thought I was going to spend their inheritance. But the person who lives day in and day out with someone who suffers from dementia or Alzheimer's is the only one who can really understand what the needs and pressures are. It may mean using some money to find a part or full time caregiver and no apologies should be made to anyone. Certainly the members of the step family should be made aware of the problems. Eventually, as others begin to have an idea of the load you have to carry; criticism will be replaced by admiration. (if you are lucky.) Norm's children had their ideas on what I should be doing but they only saw him every few months while I lived with him and his illness twenty four hours a day. This gave me a perspective no one else could have. I feel I must listen to their suggestions and then do what I know is right. As for my children and grandchildren, they have become very close to Norman and try to do all that they can to be of help. I couldn't have managed without their support.

Cut Yourself Some Slack

Don't be hard on yourself. You are entitled to lose your cool once in a while. You're not perfect so don't set standards you can't live up to. If you get impatient, your loved one will soon forget it. You won't, but don't berate yourself, it won't help anyone. A case in point, I find myself more irritable up north than I ever was in Palm Beach and though I try to hide it I'm sure he notices it. It's a combination of being responsible for too much…his finances for example…and of having no breathing room, but I mustn't let him feel it. His life is hard enough. I feel that he is aware of what's happening and often says to me, 'I'm sorry, I'm a little foggy today. I'll be better tomorrow." I assure him that he will. I don't believe it and I wonder if he does.

There is always a tendency to pamper or infantilize a person who has dementia but it is vital that Norm must do whatever is within his power to do. For instance, I let him close the car door and fasten his own seat belt, hang up his clothes, wash his hands and brush his teeth. Still I always try to be careful not to ask him to do something that will prove frustrating. It's a fine line but one I have learned to gauge and so will you.

Don't live in anticipation of changes for the worse. They will come but when they do there will be time to adjust. It isn't easy to get used to each lower level. Every time I see a further loss of comprehension I wonder how I will learn to live with it. Somehow I always do. You must live not day by day but minute to minute. I don't let myself contemplate the future and I try to celebrate every good moment.

CHAPTER ELEVEN

DIARY March 29, 1998

Last night, against my better judgment, we went to a meeting of the United Jewish Appeal. There must have been over fifty people there and most of them came over to say hello to me. Norm started to shake and I mean literally. I explained to the chairperson that we couldn't stay. Norm seemed so relieved to get into the car, but on the way home he said, "I hope I didn't embarrass you. I would never want to do that." I said, "Darling you could never embarrass me." And that is true. Sadden me, yes, embarrass me, no. Of course I didn't say that.

When we got home he fell into bed, turned to me and said, "Let's make love." It was mainly a matter of bringing him to orgasm so he went to sleep tired and happy. Of course as soon as he fell asleep I went in to the kitchen, poured myself a big glass of wine and cried quietly.

DIARY, April 23, 1998

This is the lesson I think I have finally absorbed, Norm is a very sick man with a degenerative disease and my job is to make our life together as pleasant as I can, but to stop expecting improvements that will never come. It's not an easy lesson to learn, especially for the chronic optimist I have always been, but there it is. Every once in a while the old smile lights up his face or he says something very pertinent and I'm off on my merry-go-round of hope again.

In spite of trying to stay cheerful, there are times when I do get depressed, as the following poem will show.

BIT BY BIT

I know we all must die
That we will cease to exist
It is the curse of Adam and Eve
Yet to die all at once is surely a blessing
To die bit by bit
Brain cell by brain cell
To end as a body without a mind
That is the ultimate punishment
Eve, what did I do?
Did I eat of the Tree of Knowledge?
If I did, what did I learn?
Nothing
And that is what my world has become
Empty and waiting
For what I do not know

DIARY May 27, 1998

We are living in our new small home in Westchester and I am going to a psychologist, a wonderful woman who has become my safety blanket. Sometimes it seems as if her main function is to hand me Kleenex and listen to me cry. But an important function it is. In her office I can show my true feelings and then go home to Norm and be my usual cheerful self. With her help I am now able to come to terms with sending him to a day group. In Westchester it's easy because one of his oldest friends is going to a nearby group and Norm, seeing him in the car in the morning, is happy to go. I drop in from time to time and usually find Norm dozing in a chair. He is not unhappy, but I am, since I feel that his need is for stimulation. He can sleep at home. Again I face the problem of his needs and mine and how to satisfy both.

DIARY May 18, 1998

After months of saying proudly that there has been no change I'm afraid that there has been. As usual it is not and cannot be a change for the better. Norm isn't bad during the day but he can hardly keep awake at night. Today *he came home from the group, happy but tired. I wanted him to swim but I didn't push him hard enough and acquiesced when he insisted on going to bed. When he naps too much he really gets out of it. We went to my daughter Penny's to have a cookout with her and the boys, something he loves, and he hardly said a word all evening.*

We came home and he wanted to go to bed but I turned on a nature program and he stayed up until nine. I try to keep him up at least till then.

Funny, the other night we went to an off Broadway show which went on at seven. He sat through the whole thing and though he moaned and groaned walking the three blocks back to the car he enjoyed it and today he remembered what he had seen.

I get so discouraged sometimes!!!!! But I do try not to show it. My stiff upper lip is becoming permanent. Still, I'm lucky. Once in a while Norman shows through the fog.

Almost the worst part of this illness is the loneliness. He is here, but most of the time he's asleep. Even so, I'll settle for that...and so would almost every widow I know.

CHAPTER TWELVE

I knew that little by little he was losing interest in those things that used to keep him occupied. He had been an avid bridge player and a very good one too. He started to balk at going to his usual game, a game that had been going on every Saturday for over forty years. The men Norm played with were his friends, but he began to seem frightened at the idea of playing. For a while I would drive him over and he would kibitz but eventually he refused to do even that. It was my feeling that he knew he could no longer play at his old level and was embarrassed to have the other men see it. Finally he refused to go. My free Saturday afternoons were gone. I had really treasured that time but now I would have to live without it. Another change was that Norm, formerly a voracious reader, no longer picked up a book or even a newspaper. To make him do anything I had to do it with him. He stopped doing the crossword puzzles so I would do them and ask him for the answers, which, amazingly, were nearly always forthcoming. Of course I took care to give him the easier clues so as not to make him feel inadequate.

Everyone I know who has dealt with a patient who suffers from dementia has told me that one of the most traumatic events has been telling that person they could no longer drive, and they were right. I agonized for months. How could I deprive a grown man of something he had done all his adult life? As it worked out it was easier than I expected. One morning Norm was to meet me at his office at nine thirty. Since he has always been punctual I began to worry when he hadn't arrived nine forty five. Finally at about ten minutes to ten he drove up....from the wrong direction. "What a strange thing happened," he said, "I got lost. I've been doing this drive for twenty years and all of a sudden I didn't know where I was."

I calmed him down and said he must have been thinking of something else. But that night when we were ready to drive over to a friend's house, I said, "You know darling, all these years you've been the driver and I've been the navigator. Let's swap." He agreed and got into the passenger seat. About a week later he asked, "Why are you doing all the driving lately?" "Because you don't want to drive anymore," I answered. That was the last of it. For many others explaining to a loved one that he or she can't drive anymore has been a real struggle. Still, no matter how difficult it is to take the keys away from a grown person, driving is something no dementia patient should be allowed to do, for his sake as well as the safety of others.

DIARY June 30, 1998

Everyday there are new and more important lessons to be learned and one is that I really have to be the doctor of last resort. With this disease the MDs really are just punting most of the time. I had told our doctor that Norm was jumpy and he suggested giving him a Valium every morning, which I did. The day before yesterday when I was telling my friend Grace about how much Norman slept, she asked me what he was taking. "Take him off the valium", she said, "It's making him groggy and its habit forming." So yesterday I cut the dosage in half and the difference was appreciable. From now on I'll give him a half when he feels shaky and that's all. The next thing to go is the melatonin. Let's see how he sleeps without it.

I have to remind myself that one swallow does not make a summer. One minute he is fine and I think I have my old Norm back and then he starts to shake and get disoriented. Still, I would settle to live out our lives no worse than this. He is so sweet, so patient and so loving.

DIARY July 4, 1998 Independence Day

I don't want you to think that I'm completely blasé, on Sunday the fourth I did wish, for one moment at least, that we were back in our house on the water so we could walk to the end of the dock and watch the "bombs bursting in air." But I didn't miss it enough to get into the car and drive a short distance to a friend's house where I could have watched the fireworks and have a Margarita as well.

No, my mind was not full of John Adams, Thomas Jefferson or George Washington. What I was thinking of was Norman Winik and what has happened to our storybook life. "You are so cheerful and so patient" my friends say. I answer, "I love him. How else could I be?" I do love him. And I use the present tense

DIARY July 14 1998

Rainy weekends are the worst! Norm would be happy to sleep all day and I think it's terrible for him. It's terrible for me too. Yesterday the thunder and lightning were so frightening, and although I am not usually afraid of electric storms, I let him persuade me not to make him get out of bed. He slept another hour and then I woke him and we went to a movie. I had to get him out of the house. We both enjoyed it the movie. We came home. He slept. We went out for dinner, early. We came home. I got him to watch a little TV and at eight thirty he said he was exhausted, so, you guessed it, he went to sleep.

It is now twenty minutes to ten in the morning. He got up at about seven thirty, had his cigarette, breakfast, another cigarette and now he is sleeping. It is hard being a "cruise director" and thinking of things to amuse him. As soon as I finish this I'll wake him and we'll do a little marketing. Hardly thrilling, but at least we'll get out of the house.

DIARY September 11, 1998

I guess I'll have to stop kidding myself, saying that he is holding his own. He really isn't. The deterioration is slow, but it is there. I see that puzzled frightened look more and more often and the physical tiredness is increasing. It has been almost four years since I first noticed changes so we have been lucky. There are still enough moments of "the old Norm" so I don't lose hope altogether. For instance, when the phone rings and he answers it he usually knows who is calling. His eyes brighten, his voice gets strong and he carries on a very sensible conversation. He will even make the connection to the caller by asking for the husband or the wife, and he never gets it wrong. Then he hangs up and it is as if doors have closed in his mind. He sags both physically and mentally and asks me, who called?" When I tell him it was Joe his response is always, "What about him?"

CHIAPTER THIRTEEN

At this point the casual observer could not have noticed that Norm was anything but a completely normal man. We went through all the motions of the life we had always lived. It was after an evening at a restaurant that I came home and wrote the following story.

THE HAPPIEST COUPLE

The restaurant was small. There were no more than twelve tables in all, plus an old mahogany bar. There was candlelight flickering on the white linen cloths and each table had a small flower arrangement in the center. The woman looked at the flowers and smiled, just two roses and some baby's breath, both in a bud vase. Perfect, she thought, just as the flowers in this kind of elegant restaurant usually were.

The owner knew the couple well. He greeted them by name, led them to their favorite table and without being asked, poured a glass of Pinot Grigio Santa Margarita for each of them.

The man lifted his glass and looking at the woman he smiled and said, "To my wonderful wife. I will always love you."

"To us," she replied, as they clinked their glasses and drank.

They were not young. As a matter of fact, only charity kept people from describing them as old. Old, but still handsome. He was tall with curly gray hair. large hazel eyes, high cheek bones and a strong profile. She said his nose was Roman patrician, he said it was just too big. His shoulders were broad, his waist narrow, an athlete's build. His biggest physical imperfection was that he was bow-legged. But that's an imperfection that's easily tolerated.

As for the woman, she was attractive, fairly tall, blonde and slim. Not the ravishing beauty he kept telling her she was but, as she said, "Not bad for my age."

"Darling, what should I order?" he asked. "Can I have a veal chop?"

"Of course you can," she said, After they had ordered their dinner he reached for her hand. "I adore you," he said.

It was the way it had always been. The shadow that had hung over their lives these past few years seemed to have lifted. She allowed herself a moment of hope. Maybe his illness was just a bad dream. Maybe the new drug was really a miracle cure. And then, as he smiled lovingly at her and asked, "How did we meet?" the hope was shattered, as it always was.

"You remember darling," she said, knowing that he did not or he wouldn't have asked. "I wrote you a condolence note when your wife Carolyn died and you wrote back and said you had an important question to ask me and would I call you so we could meet." How many times had they discussed this in their twenty three years of marriage? Ten thousand, twenty thousand?,? And now he couldn't remember.

"I guess I do remember vaguely," he said. "Then what happened?" he asked.

"I called you and we went out for dinner."

"Oh, that I remember. We had a lot to drink." Then with hardly a pause he asked, "Did we give the waiter the order?"

"Yes, darling. We did."

"What did we order?"

"We're splitting a prosciutto and melon and then you're having a veal chop and I'm having linguine with white clam sauce."

"Oh good, he said, "I like that." He took her hand and smiled, "Did I tell you I love you?"

"You did," she said," But you can never say it too often."

He looked worried. "Did we order?" he asked.

The waiter arrived at that moment, put down the prosciutto and melon and asked, "Pepper?"

"Not for me" he said. Then he turned to her and asked, "You'll never leave me, will you?"

"Of course not," she said, "Anyway I'm not going to get a better offer."

He seemed comforted by this and started to eat. "This is good," he said, "Did we order anything else?"

Round and round, she thought.. He asks a question. I answer. He's satisfied and then, one minute later, he asks the same question again. When there are bills to pay, this man, whose skill with numbers amazed everyone, now turns to me and asks, "Could you please help me with my checkbook?"

"Of course," she would say, "But let me get my calculator."

Where will I get the strength? she wondered. Then she looked at him and knew she would get the strength from somewhere. She had to.

When they had finished their dinner, the restaurant owner came over to the table. "Was everything to your liking?" he asked as he handed them the check.

"Everything's lovely, John" she said with a smile.

She looked at John and felt she knew what he was thinking. He was thinking that they must be the happiest couple in the world. With money, health and their obvious love for one another, what more could anyone want?

She reached for the check. "Let me do it, darling," she said.," You've forgotten your glasses." She knew he didn't really need glasses but she didn't want him to feel that she was taking over. He probably didn't notice but it was the excuse she used all the time. She put the tip on, added it up and gave it to him to sign. They got up, said goodnight to John and the happiest couple walked out of the restaurant hand in hand.

CHAPTER FOURTEEN

Norm had developed a habit which I found very disconcerting; he started picking at himself constantly. His face was covered with small bloody spots, and his arms and legs as well. I was afraid that he would get an infection. Whether this is typical of Alzheimer and dementia patients I don't know, but we had a friend who had Alzheimer's and her husband finally made her wear cotton gloves all the time. I certainly wouldn't do that with Norm, but since, all these years later, he is still picking I am always ready with peroxide and anti-biotic ointment.

At this juncture the weather started to turn cold and I thought it would be a good time to go to Florida for the winter. That way Norm could swim and be out of doors, both of which he loves. We rented an apartment sight unseen, which was fortunate, since I might not have taken it if I had seen it first. It was furnished in what I call "early Chinese nightmare." The walls were black, shiny black and hung with kimonos, and there were Buddhas of all sizes strewn around. Not knowing what awaited us, we flew down for the winter. In spite of the décor of the apartment, renting it turned out to have been a wise decision. We loved the building, the facilities and the location. Eventually we bought an apartment in the same building.

I wanted to make sure that we would have a good neurologist in Florida. Knowing that Pfizer had just developed a new drug called Aricept for dementia. I thought that they would be a good source of information and so I called Pfizer and asked for a recommendation. They suggested Dr. Carl Sadowsky, and we have been going to him ever since.

Once we were settled in I wanted to find a day group. I met with a social worker who had been recommended by the Silberstein Institute for Aging and Dementia in New York. She suggested a small group at a nearby hospital. "I've looked into it very carefully," she said, "and I think it would be a very good place for Norman."

We interviewed the woman who ran the program and she seemed understanding of Norm's problems. She had all the right credentials and a visit to the facility was reassuring. Norm said he would try it but asked, "Why can't I stay home with you?"

Seeing him go, oh so unwillingly, every morning I wondered if this was really to help him or to help me, but either way I knew that I needed a little time for myself, for both of our sakes. After a few weeks I began to have second thoughts about the group. Norm would come home with the kind of arts and crafts project my children once brought home from kindergarten, things like crepe paper flowers and colored pinwheels. Then I noticed that he was becoming more and more unresponsive. I called the understanding lady who ran the program and asked if they were medicating Norman. She said, "We are giving him Respiradol".

I had read enough to know that Respiradol was given to calm people who were having psychotic outbursts. "Why are you giving him that?" I asked.

"We want him to be a well-behaved little boy," she answered.

I could hardly control my anger. I said, "I don't. I want him to be a happy, grown up man. I'm coming right over to pick him up." I called our neurologist who was as shocked as I was. "Get him out of there," he said, "and bring him right over here. Oh yes, and throw away the Respiradol" I drove over to get Norm and started again to look for the proper facility.

The next place we tried was called Caretenders. It was housed in a building not far from where we lived. The atmosphere was cheerful and lively. The staff was warm and pleasant and the clients not too far gone into their own worlds. Norman seemed to accept going there, even if he did not exactly enjoy it. I took him in the morning and picked him up at about three, which shortened my day but seemed to leave him more cheerful. He stayed there until we went back to Westchester for the summer. There Norm returned to the group with his friend. Every time I dropped in unannounced I would find him sleeping in a reclining chair while most of the others were engaged in some sort of activity. Still I didn't make any changes. Not only was his friend there but we were going back south in a few months and it didn't seem right to change his routine for such a short time.

We had a pleasant enough summer but we were glad to get back to the south in the fall.

CHAPTER FIFTEEN

DIARY November 15, 1998

It has been raining for a week and I find that I'm beginning to be very depressed. I guess it's affecting him too. I doubled my dose of Zoloft to the level the doctor originally prescribed for me. Maybe it will help. One thing it won't do is change the reality of my life.

In spite of that Norm has had a couple of very good days. The only problem is that when that happens I let myself get so happy. I feel he has stabilized, and I let myself forget that it is only a temporary up. Decline is a constant in our lives and it's a very hard thing to live with.

DIARY January5, 1999

I have said to people that if they were sitting at dinner with him they really wouldn't notice much change. I don't think I can say that anymore. He sits at the table and stares out into space. More and more he is moving into his own world, a world in which there isn't room for anyone but himself and me. When we are alone at dinner he still manages conversation although I must take the lead. I'm a pretty voluble person but sometimes carrying the whole load can be exhausting

Yesterday a friend called to make a date. "You are so kind to call" I said," I know I should call you but I never know how people will react to Norm at this point. Not that he does anything embarrassing but he does retreat into a shell if there are more than four people at the table."

"Elaine," she said, you are our friend and Norm was our friend." Then she realized what she had said and quickly corrected herself, "Norm is our friend." The strange thing is that this was a couple I sort of inherited when I married Norm. They had been his friends and not mine

Norm IS, I screamed silently…not Norm was. Oh for heaven's sake Elaine, stop being Pollyanna the glad girl and face the truth. The core of Norm still is, the

47

sweetness, the love, the consideration. But much of what Norm was, the energy, the humor, the sense of adventure, the initiative, is gone. He asks permission to get up, to lie down. "May I go to the bathroom?" he asks, like a little boy. But he is not a boy, he is a grown man.

I'm a big one these days for homilies, I tell people that you don't look at what isn't there, and you concentrate on what is. All of a sudden, I realize that what is gets to be less and less every day. So now Mrs. Homey Philosopher, what is there to look at?

There's always the past, but that way lies sadness. I must not think of what was. If I do I'll only weep at what's been lost. How about the future? Who am I kidding? What future? I tell everyone that I don't buy green bananas. The song from Gigi where Chevalier sings, "Forevermore is shorter than before" has become my theme song.

DIARY January 11, 1999

Our friends from South Africa, whom we met going to Macchu Picchu came in this morning at 7:30 AM. It was so strange! Norm, who cannot get up before eight thirty and then says he is exhausted, jumped out of bed at six, ran into the kitchen to squeeze the juice and then insisted on driving to the airport., which he did very well except for missing the exit we always take right near our house. I, of course was giving directions, but I guess I figured he knew where he was by then and I was busy chatting with Joan. I can't take anything for granted. While it is true that he got tired during the day and had a nap both morning and afternoon he seemed much livelier than usual. He really needs something to do….but what?

DIARY March, 15, 1999

This has been a busy week. On Tuesday I had my other cataract done. At first I thought that Norm and I could manage it alone, but thank heavens I rethought that one and Penny came with us. He falls apart totally when there is any problem with me. He must have asked Penny thirty times," What are they doing to her?" While I was still conscious he asked me the same question. Penny said that as soon as I went down to the OR he fell asleep, which is his way of dealing with things.

One of the problems is that when I need a little care and pampering he can't give it and I become resentful. I know it's not his fault, I know that he loves me and would do anything for me, but at this time he hasn't the capacity. That's rationality....emotionally, I still want to be babied when I have a patch on my eye and I am still a little groggy from anesthesia. Oh well, we don't always get what we want, do we?

DIARY May 13, 1999

One very strange thing is that he doesn't seem to know he's sick. He keeps talking about two of our friends who have not been well and saying, "thank goodness we both have our health." Today he suggested that we go on a fairly rugged trip. I said that I didn't think we were fit enough. He rejected that out of hand. "We are much more active than most people of our age," he said. He who can hardly walk a block without resting. One of the few boons of this disease is lack of awareness of the reality of the situation. His lack, I'm too damned aware.

DIARY October2, 1999

Yesterday when I woke Norm up from his afternoon nap he turned to me and asked, "Are we going to Jillyflowers tonight?" Jilllyflowers, which used to be our favorite restaurant has been closed for about six or seven years. When I told him it was no longer in existence he seemed surprised and asked me about Michael, who was part owner. The whole thing was repeated about ten minutes later.

I turned on the TV to listen to the News Hour and when Ambassador Richardson came on the screen Norm said, "He looks just like King Brewster, doesn't he?" I said I had never met King. "He was best man at my wedding," he said, "How could you forget?" "I wasn't there", I said. "You weren't?" he asked, "I guess I didn't like you." This with a smile. I said, "Sweetheart, I wasn't at your first wedding." He said, "I know. I was just kidding." And he grinned. But was he? I fell apart and told me he couldn't tease me like that. It made me too nervous.

We continued dressing and, having been told at least a dozen times that we and the Hirsches were taking Ethel and Saul out to La Panatiere for their fiftieth anniversary, he asked, "Are we going out with Harry and Norma?" "Norma is dead, darling." I said. "Oh, but why not Harry? Harry is my good friend." By this time all I wanted was a shot of Demerol....or something.

I drove to the restaurant and as we went in he looked around in a sort of surprised way and said, "This isn't Jillyflowers. It's La Panatiere." That's probably more than he said at dinner. As soon as the others came he retreated to some private place and only emerged to eat lots of rolls and butter and three kinds of dessert. There was stuff in between but most of it came home with us in a doggy bag. As soon as we got into the car he became chatty again.

DIARY November 4, 1999

Wednesday we went to see Dr. Libow and he was very pleased with Norm. Said he was "stable". And he seemed to be, but you can't tell from one minute to the next how he is going to be. Yesterday we went to see our old housekeeper Mima, who hasn't been well. Then we went swimming. We had hot dogs at the wagon on Purchase Street...Norm's favorite...and then he agreed to come to Nordstrom's to buy a pair of desperately needed shoes. He was in his usual after-swim mood, which is up and with it. Of course ten minutes in the store and the veil descended. He asked to be allowed just to sit down. Which of course he did while I ran around and got him a shirt and some socks. We were out of there, with shoes, in half an hour.

We came home and he went to sleep. The hours between three and six thirty are the hardest for me. He sleeps and I skulk around looking for things to do. I usually wake him an hour before I have to, so he has time to get oriented. Sometimes he does and sometimes he doesn't. None of this is his fault. I wonder how much he realizes about how he has changed. I hope he doesn't. It's enough that I do.

DIARY November 9, 1999

We went out to dinner by ourselves last night. After we were seated and Norm was served the first of his many Cokes, he asked me, "Did we order?" I said we hadn't but I signaled the waiter and ordered for both of us. He no longer wants to choose his own food but tells me to do it. One minute later he asked, "Did we order

yet?" *over and over, "Did we order?" "What did we order" and a new scary one, after looking around the restaurant, "What are we doing here?"*

The worst was yet to come. I now add the check and put on the tip. I always ask Norm how much first and then give him the check to sign. He took it and it was almost as if he had forgotten how to sign his name. he sort of printed "NOR-MAN" in shaky characters, then seemed to recover a little on the "Winik" and wrote it almost the way he usually does with the exception of a lovely loop over the W. That wasn't there. All night long I could see that signature in front of my eyes.

Diary December 20, 1999

The new apartment here in Florida is much nicer than last year's, and we are where we should be at this stage of our lives. When we arrived the men downstairs greeted us with "Welcome home," which made us feel good. It is as if we had never left. My friends Leona and Judy were at the pool, Natalie was around the corner, Grace, Tubby and Ellie, (my surrogate family) are all here for us.

Monday we go to see Dr. Sadowsky, the neurologist and then on Tuesday I start my interviews for another group for him. Caretenders, his day group, has moved to a new location which is at least a half hour drive, and more than that in traffic. I knew that he must have more stimulation than I could give him. It would be good for both of us if we each had a different destination for part of the day. The strange thing is that I have devoted myself so completely to him for the past few years that I'll have to relearn how to live my own life. It even scares me a little but there's no sense worrying until I see if there is a group suitable for Norm. When we find it, and I know we will, I'll look around for some courses to take and maybe even learn to play bridge.

DIARY January 3, 2000

Norm is constantly picking at his face and at his ears. He looks as if he's been in a fight with a cat. I worry about infection since he is not too careful about washing his hands. I'm always at the ready with peroxide and antibiotic ointment. He agrees to stop, but of course he forgets in about two seconds. Today I wrote him a note that said, "NORM HAS TO STOP PICKING OR HE WILL GET AN

INFECTION AND ELAINE WILL GO NUTS!!!" It will probably work for about ten minutes.

Needless to say I thought the whole thing over and never gave him the note.. It wouldn't have helped and it might have been belittling

---

DIARY January13, 2000

I learned something very important this week. Lately Norm has been telling me that he is so dizzy and faint that he must lie down at once. As a rule I let him do it. Three days ago I tried a new tack. When he started his, by now, routine plea, I said in quite a severe voice, "You are not going to faint. You just want to get back to bed and hibernate. I'm not going to let you. So take a deep breath, pull yourself together and let's go." He grinned sheepishly and we went out. I'll keep doing this as long as it works.

One piece of encouraging behavior was that he walked to the pool at the next building by himself while I was taking my computer lesson. It's the first time he has done anything alone since we got here. He does seem to like it in Florida. Our social life is busy, last night we went to dinner and concert with Natalie Stone. In retrospect he says he enjoyed it, but today when I tried to wake him from his nap so we could get dressed and go out he said he was sick and "disoriented". That has become a sort of pattern. I wake him. He says he feels awful. I say that we can stay home. He says he'll make it and he does...not with his old exuberance, but at least he tries. One thing he has hung on to is his sweetness, he must tell me twenty times a day how much he loves me and knows what I am doing for him. This is a very hard time, but that does make it easier and life is better for us here. I am convinced that we made a smart move in coming here for the winter.

CHAPTER SIXTEEN

It was at this time that I realized that the pain in my knee had become so severe that I had to have a knee replacement. I would have to be in the hospital for four days and basically off my feet for three weeks. What would I do about Norm? A friend recommended a male nurse who could stay with Norm and my daughter Penny came down to look after me. I went to the hospital not realizing how debilitating the procedure would be. It was so terribly painful that I could hardly muster a smile for Norm when my daughter Penny brought him to the hospital to visit. As it turned out, this knee replacement was one of the great blessings of my life. Not only was I finally out of pain but more important than that, it brought Linda into our lives.

DIARY January 16, 2000

Norm has gotten so used to Linda, the wonderful nurse's aide who came to take care of me while I was recovering from my surgery, that he is willing to go to the pool with her and to leave me at home. What a relief to have a little time to myself and to have someone who can keep Norm busy when I am unable to. To find someone trustworthy and kind who can spell you, is finding the greatest treasure. Caregivers represent security to someone with dementia and the primary caregiver cannot be on duty twenty-four hours a day…every day. I hope that she stays with us for a while, at least until I feel stronger.

What a blessing, Linda has said she will come back to New York with us and that will make my life so much easier…

DIARY February 18, 2000

Day before yesterday I woke Norm up from his nap and he began to shake violently. I said, "Sweetheart, we are going out for dinner.

He said, "I'm so dizzy." Then he sat up, looked at me angrily and said, "I'm going to start driving again. You never take me anywhere."

"Where do you want to go that I don't take you?" Then before he could answer I asked, "were you having a bad dream?" He shook his head yes and the subject was forgotten. He does do a lot of dreaming and from what he has said in his sleep and upon waking up, I'm sure that those dreams are both realistic and violent. Poor guy, even resting is not restful for him anymore.

DIARY March 18, 2000

My computer has been on the blink for about a week, so I couldn't write. I now have a new one that I'm still getting used to, and believe me, at this age, it isn't easy. Norm seems all right except just before dinner. He wakes up from his nap he is so groggy and shaky. The conversation goes round and round. "Are we going out with the big fella tonight?" he asks.

"No darling." He's dead"

Look of shock followed by, "When did he die?"

"About six months ago."

"What did he die of?"

"He was on dialysis for twenty years. His kidneys just gave out."

A few moments of silence and then, "Are we going out with the big fella tonight?"

I tell myself, "PATIENCE" and I'm proud to say that most of the time I manage not to show my frustration.

DIARY April 14, 2000

Norm also asks which Marine buddy is coming for dinner tonight. That has now been augmented by which kid he went to school with. When he asks if "Poppy" is going to have dinner with us and I ask, "Who is Poppy?" he looks shocked and says, "You remember Poppy. He went to prep school with me." This gambit, with a change of names is repeated over and over. It can be exhausting just trying to stay patient. I'm not a candidate for sainthood but I do try to stay calm and most of the time I manage.

Norm has been asking more and more frequently if he is going to the Marine base today. When I tell him he isn't going, he says, "But I'm still in the Marines, aren't I?" I usually answer him by saying that the Marine Corps doesn't take almost eighty year old men. He laughs and then asks me if Hoss Moss or some other Marine Corps buddy is coming for dinner. When he mentions a name I don't recognize and I ask him who he's talking about, he looks at me with amazement. "You remember him," he says. "We were at the base at Laguna together." I remind him that he was married to Carolyn then and not to me. He usually nods and accepts that. I have always dreaded that the day would come when Norm calls me Carolyn. (So far it hasn't.) But one day the following took place.

"Are we meeting Carolyn for lunch?" He asked.

"My heart stopped. "Carolyn who?" I asked.

"You know," he answered. "Carolyn, my wife."

"Darling, she's dead. If she were alive we wouldn't be married."

He gave me a quizzical look and said, "I know she's dead and you are my wife. What are you talking about?"

Maybe it's not a roller coaster I'm on. Sometimes it feels more like a seesaw.

DIARY, April 27, 2000

Tonight we went to Murray and Charlotte Peter's house for dinner. Norm was very shaky and almost fell asleep at the table. We left right after dinner and he slept in the car on the way home. He stumbled through the lobby, almost bumping against the walls. I wonder if we'll have to give up going out at night.

The night before last went out with Leona and Marcy. Norm, after a bad beginning when we were leaving our apartment, was just incredible. He was funny, cute and with it. Today he was the same. Of course, eternal optimist that I am, I thought he was getting better. Today we went to Loxahatchee to bird-watch, then we had lunch and swam. I was on a high. We came back to the apartment, he napped, and by the time we left for dinner he was dizzy and shaky. I did the driving and he clung to me. It is now nine o'clock and he is fast asleep. Tomorrow I'll call all over to see about the Aricept.

DIARY April 21, 2000

Yesterday Norm turned to me and said, "Darling, I'm so sorry."

"Sorry about what?" I asked.

"Sorry that I'm so vague."

That was the first time in a long while that he has given any sign that he knows anything is wrong with him. Certainly he has no clue that he is constantly asking me if he is going to his squadron tomorrow, or that we run the gamut of his dead friends at dinner.

"Is Harry dead?"

"Yes darling. He died last year."

"Is Walter dead?"

"For about thirty years." And on and on it goes. Today I almost lost my patience with him, and then I looked at his sad face

"It must be hard not to remember." I said.

He nodded and I told him that he always had me to remind him of the details. That seemed to comfort him. He understood I think, but I am never sure of how much he really takes in.

CHAPTER EIGHTEEN

DIARY August 3, 2000

Norm's daughters were here yesterday, and as usual they got to me. They wanted to take him out for lunch. I agreed but asked them to bring him back before 3:00, as he hadn't been feeling too well. Agreed? Agreed. By 4:15 I was a nervous wreck, maybe they had been in an accident.....maybe....who knows what.

They finally cam home just before 5:00. Norm looked absolutely exhausted. It seems they had some shopping to do and so they took him with them. Of all the things Norm hates, shopping is number one. Mary said that they had had "a lot of fun." But when we were alone Norm said he hadn't wanted to go and had told them so. I guess it won't kill him, and they did all their own errands. Still I find it hard to believe that they let their interests come before their father's well-being. I guess only someone living with a dementia patient can really gauge their feelings.

DIARY October 10, 2000

Quite often now, he will say, "I don't know what's the matter with me. I'm so out of it." And he is, more and more. Still he can still hold his own in small groups. He doesn't really participate, but he can fake it. The shakiness and the tiredness seem to be on the increase.

As for me, I'm on the edge of despair. If he knew how sad his illness makes me, he would really go crazy.

DIARY December 10, 2001

This has been a bad week. I guess, from now on each week will be a little worse than the one before, and I'll just have to learn to live with it. Norm has become more and more dependent and would sleep all day long if we would let him. Have I said that before? The difference may be that I feel I'm on the brink of a depression and find it harder and harder to cope with our problems.

Wednesday we went out to dinner with our friends Bobbie and Sidney Stayman. We were having a pleasant time when all of a sudden I felt a wave of nausea. I got up from the table, said I didn't feel well and that I wanted to go outside and get a breath of fresh air. I don't think I fainted, but I came close. I stood outside the restaurant and retched. I felt very light-headed. Poor Norm was terrified. He wanted to drive me home, but bless Bobbie, she said he was too upset to drive and that she would drive me. Sid drove Norm. I think it must have been some kind of intestinal virus. The next day I felt better, if still a little weak and much less depressed than I had been. Thank God for my optimistic nature, I don't seem to stay down very long.

DIARY December 20, 2000

We stayed home for dinner on Thursday. Norm was sitting in front of the T.V. with his dinner on a folding table when he turned to me and asked, "What are we doing in this room?" My heart hit bottom and I asked, "What do you think we're doing, darling?" "Eating dinner." he said with a smile. But he had been confused enough to ask the question.

DIARY January 18, 2001

Tonight I just didn't feel like cooking, even a light supper and so we went out for a lovely dinner. Actually the dinner wasn't that great but we sat outside on a terrace where it was cool and QUIET (!) something that's hard to find in Palm Beach. The wine was delicious and someone else served it and someone else washed the dishes. What a pleasure! We are both happy when we are out together and Norm smiles a lot and tells me how much he loves me. So if the food wasn't sensational. I don't really give a damn. At this time of my life, food is not that important to me..

DIARY February 4 2001,

I try to take Norm and Linda to the exercise classes, which they have here every day. Not only is it good for him but it seems to be good for me as well. He sits behind me...Linda sits next to him and I smile at him in the mirror. When he is not smiling back he has a totally blank look on his face. Still he manages to do some of the drills, and I figure whatever little he does is better than nothing. I've noticed that as the days go by he seems to do a bit more each time. It sounds like a terrible thing to say, but if nothing else it helps to pass the day. The more we can program him the less he sleeps and smokes.

DIARY February 20, 2001

Yesterday we went to see Dr. Sadowsky, the neurologist. He "examined" Norm very perfunctorily, asked him a few questions, "What year is it?" "1996", "Who is president?" "Clinton", "Who was just elected?" "I don't know" etc. We discussed the effects of Exelon and he said that Norm was on a minimal dosage and he upped the quantity. We will see.

DIARY February 27, 2001

My heart is breaking! The change in the last few days has been terrifying. Norm is so dizzy that I'm always afraid he'll fall. The questions he asks are getting more and more bizarre, for instance, I handed him his shoes and socks and told him to put them on. He looked at me and asked, "Which do I put on first?" I said, "Which do you think?" And he did it properly. But he has so little confidence that he asks me what to do about everything.

Tonight Stanley and Barbara were here for dinner. He is very comfortable with them and yet he was totally removed all through dinner. Every once in a while, as if from nowhere, he would chime in with the answer to something we were discussing...he was always right on the mark...and then he would lapse back into his own world. I live in fear of the day when he retreats into that world and can't find his way back. I tell myself not to anticipate, that it will come soon enough…but then I'm constantly giving myself all kinds of good and gratuitous advice, some of which I sometimes take.

DIARY March 10, 2001

By the way, I had taken him off Ritalin because I didn't think it had any effect, but I now realize that without it he sleeps a great deal more, so I have put him back on it. Dr. Elaine. At this point I feel as if I am doctor, care giver, lover, event planner, jack of all trades, master of none.

Diary April 17, 2001

She was a lovely lady, small, very old and quite homely. I never saw the homeliness because her face was always wreathed in smiles and when she spoke to you, you felt that you were the most important person in the world to her. We weren't close friends but we had had dinner together on more than a few occasions. Yet every time we met her I was nervous. I knew what Norm's reaction would be. "Who is that ugly lady?" he would ask. I would give him a poke, hope she hadn't heard. Luckily she was well past ninety and a little hard of hearing.

Once she had walked on, still smiling, I would say to Norm, "Darling wait 'till the footsteps die before you make comments about people."

He would nod and then say, "But she really is ugly. Who is she?" When we see a particularly fat person on the street I steer Norm in the other direction as fast as I can so if he comments, no one will hear but me.

"Wow! Will you look at that ass" he will say, not whisper, as I try to look the other way.

DIARY May 27, 2001

Poor Norm, I haven't been feeling well and he can't understand my being sick. He has gotten so used to being waited on. Linda will be standing over me and massaging my knee with ice, Norm stands there and says, "I'd like a cigarette NOW." The illness has made him totally self-centered.

Norm had been a smoker for years. About the fourth year of our marriage he finally decided to give it up. He went to a place called Smokenders and finally broke the habit. He stopped smoking for sixteen years. Then about a year after the start of his dementia he began to ask for a cigarette, especially after breakfast. I've never been a smoker and so I have a hard time understanding his need, but I soon realized that the cigarette could be a kind of carrot. The following became our routine.

Norm would wake up and ask, "Can I have a cigarette now?"

"Finish your breakfast first."

"And then can I have one?"

"Of course, darling." He has so few real pleasures left that it's hard to deny him two or three cigarettes a day. After breakfast he goes out on the deck and smokes with a look of absolute peace on his face. Tobacco may be an evil, but in his case it's a sort of blessing.

Since his long term memory is still quite sharp I suggested to him that he should dictate his memories of World War 11 and that I would write them up. He had been a Marine Corps captain, a dive bomber pilot in the Pacific theater and had seen a great seal of action. The idea excited him, and as few things excited him anymore, we spent hours on the project, usually at the pool. He would reminisce and I would take it all down on my laptop. An ancillary benefit was that the Marine Corp was looking for first person reminiscences and so his story is now on record in Washington D.C. Of course his memories of those long-ago days were fresh and clear.

CHAPTER NINETEEN

It was about this time when I noticed that certain people who I had thought were very good friends, began to fall away. I realized then that the specter of dementia haunts a great many people as they approach old age. It isn't contagious, I thought, and I was shocked at those who acted as if it were. At first I was hurt and angry that some people we used to see almost every week were suddenly too busy to meet us, especially since Norm is never a source of embarrassment. I admit that he doesn't add to the conversation. On the other hand I can talk enough for two. Sometimes I feel as if I have to, and that can be exhausting.

A COUNTRY OF STRANGERS

Where have they gone?
All the dear devoted friends
They surrounded me when life was good
They laughed with me when I could be part of the gaiety
It will always be this way they said
Friendship is forever
Now they are not here to dry the tears
And I am alone
In a country of strangers

Dementia is a disease of losses. I have spoken of the loss of energy and of skills, but one of the saddest losses is the loss of confidence. To see a person who once ran a successful business and made executive decisions asking permission to go to the bathroom or to lie down is heartbreaking. It does no good to say," Darling, you know you don't have to ask me that." In a few minutes you'll be asked a very similar question. Don't explode. Take a deep breath and answer. Remind yourself for the umpteenth time that he doesn't remember and that he doesn't mean to be difficult.

I seem to be infinitely patient with Norm, which is strange since I have never been noted for that trait. I remember when my youngest child came home from third grade and told me that they were studying adjectives. "We had to give an adjective for each of our family," she said. I asked what she had given her dad and her siblings, and then, "What did you use for me?" She looked at me with a grin and said, "impatient."

DIARY September 16, 2001

This afternoon he must have asked me forty times where and with whom we were going to dinner. I finally said, "I just told you, darling, don't you remember?" When he came up with the right answer I asked him why he kept asking me if he knew the answer. He said, "I'm sorry, I get mixed up and I forget." The look on his face was so sad that I could have killed myself for asking.

I remembered that at the beginning of Norm's illness that I asked him, "Why do you keep asking me that question?" He looked at me with such sadness and said, "Because I just can't remember." I promised myself never to ask that question again. Apparently I needed to be reminded.

Diary October 31, 2001

Today is Norm's eightieth birthday. I can't believe it, and I don't think he is really aware of it. Still, today when someone asked him how it felt to be eighty years old he said, "Exactly the same as it feels to be seventy-nine." He still comes up with a germane answer every once in a while...

DIARY November 7, 2001

When I woke him from his afternoon nap he was so dizzy that he said he couldn't get up. He seemed totally confused and was holding one hand down on his right leg to keep it from shaking. I said, "Darling, we don't have to go to the restaurant. I've got enough in the house for dinner." He said he would try to get dressed if I would help him. I did, wondering if I was doing the right thing. After about the half hour it took to get him dressed, we went downstairs, walked the half block to the restaurant and again he was a perfectly normal man. The great problem is that by the time I pull him together I'm ready to fall apart.

So how hard do you push? That is the question we all live with. The brain is a muscle and needs to be exercised….at least that's what I tell myself. So I try to keep him as active as I can. It's like walking a tightrope, which is not my favorite sport. Still I'm getting quite good at it. Amazing what practice can do.

Grandchildren can be a big help. I wrote this in my diary after Jill and Ben came to visit.

Diary February 18, 2002

Jill just left after a visit of four and a half days. She is delightful. On Friday evening she and we were joined by Ben. What fun we had. They are so full of ideas and so sweet besides. Their parents should be proud of them. I know their grandparents are. I really loved having them here. Although when Ben arrived we shipped them to the hotel down the street, not only so I could have my bathroom back but also because I thought they would love the chance to be together…they did. Still I must admit that I feel as if I can't get caught up. Linda was sick on Wednesday so I had to take Norm to the airport to pick Jill up. He gets a little baffled whenever he does anything outside of his routine so he gave her a very lukewarm welcome. But when we got back to our own apartment he hugged her and gave one of his wonderful smiles. They've been in love since the day they met.

DIARY March 25, 20002

Norm now has the most vivid dreams, not always nightmares just vivid. Last night he woke me up asking, "Do you think Ike will win?" "Ike who" I asked. "Ike Eisenhower of course," he said and went back to sleep. I didn't have a clue where that came from.

DIARY Wednesday, April 19, 2002

I've just come up from doing water aerobics with Norm and Linda. The last few days have not been particularly good ones. He wants to do NOTHING but sleep and smoke. We can manage to get him in the water for about thirty-five minutes, during which I keep him and myself...moving. He is always at his best when he's in the pool. I know the circulation is better when he's moving, the problem is that it's so hard to get him to do anything. We keep trying. Linda says she thinks he's depressed and as we can never get the doctor on the phone, we have increased some of his medications on our own. They are all medications that have been approved and prescribed by his doctor. Linda and I have decided that we know more about his reactions than anyone else. So we sometimes juggle the medication a little bit. At one point it became hard to keep him awake and we cut down on his Paxil, with very good results..

I'm not a doctor, and I wondered how our neurologist would react when we told him. His answer both surprised and comforted me. "Each case is so different," he said, "and you live with him so you have a good idea about the effects of each medication." The he added, with a smile, "but don't make a habit of it."

Norm's finger trick in Brazil

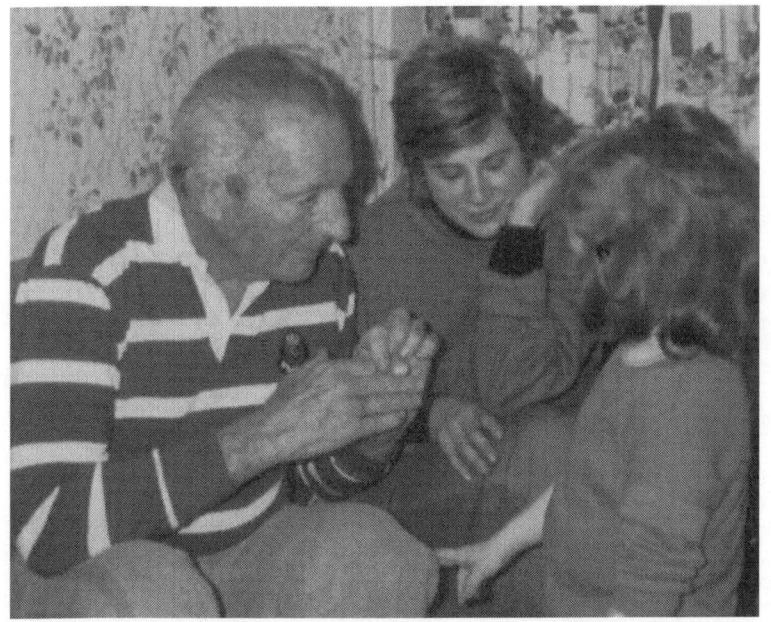

The finger trick in Moscow

Sailing off the Greek Islands

The long walk to the toilet in Alaska

Norm and some local belles in Kenya

Norm feeding me in Svaalbard, northern Norway

"Our park" in Jerusalem

In front of the Knesset (parliament) Jerusalem

One of our many plumbing problems, the Grand Tetons

CHAPTER TWENTY

DIARY June 3 2002

What a scary experience I had this morning! It was like a scene from the movie Awakenings. Norm woke me at7 A.M. and started to ask the most cogent questions. He asked me whether or not we had a mortgage on the new house. I told him no and he asked if we had one on this apartment. When I said we did, he wanted to know for how much and at what rate of interest. He was pleased with the rate. He asked if I wasn't going north this week to work on the new house. Then he started to insist that he go with me. "After all," he said, "we are partners and we do things together."

"What airline did you book?" was the next question, followed by "Call Delta and book a ticket for me." He repeated the last about five times, to make sure I would understand that he was serious about it.

He was also interested in how much money he had and with whom it was invested. When I told him that it was with Northern Trust and showed him the records, he started to ask for things that had been in his bedside table and desk at our old house in Rye. He asked for each individual thing and then wanted to know if there would be room for a desk for him in the new house. I showed him the plans, for the fiftieth time, this time he seemed to absorb it. "It looks very nice," he said," But won't the outside be a little dull with so many similar houses all around it?" I must admit that he was not wrong. It certainly wasn't the beautiful house we had just sold but it was smaller and would be cheaper and easier to maintain.

When Linda came in he told her in a loud clear voice that he was a grown man and not a child and would do his showering and shaving without her "hanging over" him.

He had just finished telling me the same thing. Having said it he went into the bathroom showered and shaved and came out with a big smile on his face.

I was much more frightened than elated. I knew it was not a miracle and I was scared that he would become argumentative. He had certainly been so on the subject of going north with me. I reminded him that he had just gotten over a long, lingering cold and that it might be too soon to fly. He answered me by saying that if I had given him Nyquil instead of some other cough syrup he would have stopped coughing long ago. "You don't know what a wonderful medication Nyquil is," he assured me. "We must go to Green's Drug Store and buy some. I'll drive. There is no reason why I shouldn't drive, is there? And while we're talking, I don't want to beg for a cigarette. I'll keep a pack and take one when I want it." All this and more was said in a strong voice, not the sort of wheedling baby voice I've gotten used to. All in all it was incredible, but I couldn't see it as an improvement, only trouble. It was too good to be true and I couldn't allow myself to get my hopes up.

By lunchtime it was over. When I said we were going to Green's to get Nyquil, he looked puzzled and asked why we needed Nyquil. Then he wanted to know what the plans for the evening were, and if he could lie down and if he could have a cigarette.

I began to have crazy thoughts, like the idea that all of his violent coughing the last few days had shaken something loose in his brain. Coming to my senses, I was almost relieved to have the amenable, sleepy Norman back! Not that I wouldn't give everything I have in the world to see him well, but I'm too much of a realist to believe that could happen and I only foresaw him refusing to go to his day group and my losing what little freedom I had. What a weird and awful disease.

DIARY November 23, 2002

I know that I should live for those moments when Norm is Norm. They are few and far apart these days and I am certain that it will get worse. In spite of that knowledge, when he gives me one of his bright smiles I'm buoyed up....for a little while at least.

I feel that we must have some social life so I accepted a date with some new acquaintances that live here in the building. The man has very advanced Parkinson's and can hardly speak. He can't cut his food and he shakes. What fun the evening was! Norm is getting more and more vague, he will look at a sweater I have just given him to put on and ask, "What's this?" So between the two men…and the other woman, who hardly said a word, I felt obliged to keep the conversation going and by the time we got home I was exhausted. I've got to get over the feeling that I must be the life of the party.

Diary January 21 2003

He was so out of it today. He slept after lunch and then I dragged him out to see a movie. I had picked what I thought would be a good movie, but it turned out to be so slow that even I was anxious to leave, and we did, after about an hour and a half. We came back to the restaurant in the building. It is so easy to get there and as he was feeling so shaky, I thought it would be the best place to go. On Friday and Saturday night they have a pianist and singer who play "our music". All of a sudden Norm woke up and began to sing along, making sad faces when the lyrics were about unrequited love, and in general mugging as he sang. I was laughing hysterically, partly from joy at seeing him so engaged, and partly because he was so cute.

In the car I play CDs of Bing Crosby and Frank Sinatra, old songs that I know he will remember. Very often he will start to sing along. He always knows all the words and the two of us sing happily, if off-key.

Diary March 10, 2003

As Norm's illness moves, inexorably, but thank heavens slowly, one great change emerges in clear definition; his world is getting smaller and smaller. This man, who always had such consideration for others, is now able just to think of his own wants and needs. We can be sitting in a restaurant and everyone else at our table is eating his or her main course. He has finished all that he wants so he calls the waiter over and asks for ice cream. It's not rudeness, it's just that he hasn't got the capacity to see beyond himself. When I tell him to wait for the rest of us to finish, he makes a face, but, as he always does, he listens to me. However I don't think he really understands why I'm frustrating him. It's the same thing when he eats roll after roll, thickly, and I really mean thickly, smeared with butter. I try to make him stop because the doctor has said that butter is bad for his high cholesterol. So now there's a choice between cholesterol and frustration. I usually solve it by asking everyone at the table if they want any more bread and if they don't, I ask the waiter to take it away. At home it is simpler, I just don't serve it. If he doesn't see it, he doesn't want it.

We go home to New York in a month and except for the fact that Linda will be away for a month (!) I'm looking forward to the change. God bless the Zoloft. I walk around feeling happy most of the time. Truth to tell, with Norm so sweet, my family and Linda so wonderful, I do feel relaxed most of the time. There are things I miss, going to Israel, travel in general, the long talks we used to have and most of all, the Norman that was, but I don't dwell on it. I've had this wonderful marriage on loan I guess, so I settle for what is.

I have said that I consider myself lucky because Norm never does anything embarrassing in public. Memory can help us hide what we don't want to face, and the following incident is one I can certainly understand wanting to forget. On rereading my diary I was almost shocked to remember it.

March 2 3, 2003

It was raining today so I brought Norm to a nearby mall where he could take a walk. We had stopped to get an ice cream cone, which he loves, and started to walk toward the parking garage. Suddenly he looked down and called out in a horrified tone, " What is that on my leg?" I took a quick look and realized that he had soiled himself. I was panicked and began to look for the nearest men's room. Then I realized that I couldn't go in with him and that he wouldn't know what to do without me. I was trying to calm both of us down when I heard a voice behind me saying, "I think I can help you." I turned around to see a small, well dressed woman of about my age. "I've been through this with my husband," she said. "I live nearby. You can follow me to my house, give him a shower and I'll lend you a pair of my husband's pants."

I don't usually follow absolute strangers but at that moment I would have followed anyone who offered to help. We got into our car. She got into hers and we followed her for about five minutes. She stopped in front of a small, neat, pale beige stucco house. She opened the door and showed us into the bathroom where I was able to clean Norm up, all the while telling him that accidents happened to everybody. Our rescuer called in," There are some clothes just outside the door for your husband." She said. I opened the door and found a pair of clean underpants and beige chinos.

When we got out of the bathroom I thanked her profusely and asked for her name and address so I could return the pants. Her answer came quickly. "Don't worry about returning them. My husband is gone and doesn't need them anymore. As for thanking me, don't. Anyone who has been in this position is more than happy to help. Just take him home and be glad he is still with you."

I did just that, but instead of crying about what had happened to Norm and to me, I felt privileged to have met a person of such generosity of spirit. I wish I had insisted on getting her name so I could at least have sent her flowers. I suppose the only real way to thank her is for me to help someone else in need.

April 10, 2003

Today is the worst kind of day…. a rainy Saturday. It is exacerbated by the fact that I've got a nasty cold and don't feel well at all. So we can't go outside and swim, neither of us feels like going to a movie and I'm having a severe attack of cabin fever. Maybe I don't have the right to complain since we did meet friends at the Yacht Club for lunch which broke up the day a little. I'm also reading a good book about the United Jewish Appeal. It brings back so very many memories of the days when I was active.

You can see that I'm trying to count my blessings…but I don't think I've convinced myself that I'm the luckiest woman in the world. To add to that I'm not using this seemingly endless day to do something creative. Instead after every few chapters I put down my book and play Solitaire on the computer, do a crossword puzzle or try to find something interesting on the TV. (A lost cause.) Norm of course sleeps through it all, which is probably the smartest thing to do on a rainy Saturday.

CHAPTER TWENTY ONE

SEX

One can almost hear the unasked question. Is he still interested in sex? The answer in our case is yes…or should I say, yes, but. In the early years of the dementia he was not only interested but very virile and still maintained his interest in pleasing me. As time passed he was less and less able to maintain an erection and his desire became simply to bring himself to orgasm. What kept me from going wild with frustration was the fact that even at these times he would tell me that he loved me.

If we make love just before we fall asleep Norm is likely to wake me at about two A.M., stroking me and telling me to stroke him. I'm not complaining, but what used to be a wonderful exciting experience has become an exercise in giving him an outlet. Knowing that's what it is, I try to say yes unless it is really inopportune, for instance when we have just gotten dressed and are ready to go out. If we are pressed for time I dress in the closet so as not to turn him on. Most women of my age would love to have this problem, I know and at least it makes me feel as if I'm desirable.

Finally I decided that for both of our sakes that I would give him Viagra. The doctor agreed that it couldn't hurt. So on a rainy Sunday, late in the afternoon (I was told it took two to three hours to work.) I gave him a Viagra pill and told him it was a vitamin. He dutifully took it, asked for something to eat and then went to bed and slept soundly till the next morning. I had the choice of laughing or crying. I laughed.

I know that I sound like a Pollyanna but I am not young and to me the caress, the words and the loving look are infinitely more precious than sex itself. Not that I don't miss it but this is what I've got and there is no use in dwelling on what I no longer have. Anyone I know who has lost a spouse would change places with me. For all the losses I still have my husband here where I can touch him. The empathy, which was one of his strongest traits, has gone. This disease forces its victims to concentrate on themselves just to maintain their equilibrium, but the love remains. In that as in so much else, one learns to work with that.

I have looked through all of my diaries for a record of the following incident and I can't find it. Perhaps it was too painful for me to write about. However it is so etched into my mind that I will never forget it.

It was a Saturday sometime in the winter of 2004. Linda was out and Norm and I were just finishing breakfast. It must have been about nine-thirty" when Norm turned to me and said, "I have to go to the bathroom". I told him to go ahead. He had always taken himself to the bathroom so I just went on reading the New York Times. What made me go into the bathroom to check on him I will never know, but something told me to do it. I walked in to see him on the toilet with his head against the wall and his eyes rolled up in his head. He looked like a corpse. I tried to get him off the toilet but he slid to the floor. Somehow I had the presence of mind to call 911. It was only minutes until the paramedics arrived. I was absolutely calm. I think I was in a state of shock. I went through the paces like an automaton.

The emergency medics put an oxygen mask on his face, took his vital signs and got him onto a stretcher....maybe not in that order but I can be forgiven if I don't remember the exact details. "We're taking him to Good Sam" (Good Samaritan the nearest hospital) one of them said. "He is breathing normally".

Thank heavens for that I thought. I was about to ask if I could come in the ambulance when I thought I that once Norm settled in I might need the car to come home and get him some things. "I'll follow you," I said. Mistake number one, as I found when I get to the hospital just as the ambulance was pulling in.

I explained to the nurse at the emergency room desk that I had to go in to be with my husband. I said that he had a dementia and would be terrified if he woke up in a strange place and didn't see me there. She was not impressed. "Sit down and wait until he is admitted or discharged." What could I do? I sat down and started to figure out how I could get into the emergency room. Luck was with me. I was sitting forlornly, wondering what to do when a neighbor of mine came into the hospital seeing me he walked over. "What are you doing here?" he asked. I explained the situation and he said, "I'm a volunteer here, come on, I'll get you in."

I bless him every time I think of that day, especially when I remember the look on Norm's face when he saw me. "What am I doing here darling?" he asked and I was able to reassure him.

While I was outside I had called Linda and she came as quickly as she could. She must have passed every red light in town. The two of us sat by his bedside in the emergency room until about four in the afternoon when he was finally admitted. The doctors said it was a "vagal incident" which I found out meant that he was exerting too much pressure trying to move his bowels. They said it wasn't serious but they wanted him in the hospital for a few days.

His room was pleasant and even had a terrace which Norm never used, but which I would occasionally go out on to get a breath of air. Linda insisted on sleeping in the room with him that night. I went home, reassured my family and friends…news spreads quickly when an ambulance comes to the front door of our apartment house…and fell into a deep sleep.

Three days later we brought him home, in perfect health. He doesn't remember a thing about it, but I can still see his eyes rolled up and now I always take a look at him when he is going to the bathroom.

Humor

Before I married Norm I thought about what would be the most important traits a future husband could have. I came up with three which I felt were absolutely necessary, They were, 1. A sense of humor, 2. A sense of humor and 3.…you guessed it…a sense of humor. The ability to laugh, especially at oneself was vital to me. Norm had the most wonderful sense of humor and we spent a lot of time sharing things we found amusing. About five years into this illness I began to realize that Norm seemed to be losing his formerly acute sense of humor. But as I learn over and over, one can never be sure of anything.

The other day, ten years into his dementia, we were walking down the street. Norm had a look of intense pain on his face. "Darling," I said," don't look so pathetic. Everyone has problems. Even I have a problem."

"What's your problem?" he asked.

"You," I said with a smile. He started to laugh just as he would have ten years ago. As I say over and over, one never knows.

Simplify but Don't Infantilize

It's so important not to infantilize a person with dementia. Whatever skills he may retain should be put to use, but try to simplify whenever you can. About five years ago I started picking out Norm's clothes and placing them where it would be easy for him to dress himself. He no longer wears lace-up shoes. Tying the laces might confuse him and there are plenty of good slip-on styles.…to say nothing of Velcro. Open neck sport shirts present no problem, once in a while we are invited to a dinner where men are required to wear a tie.…..now that is a hassle.

Norm hates the feeling of constriction so I try to avoid those evenings whenever possible. On the other hand I try to make him do whatever he can manage by himself. Friends often try to help him fasten his seat belt and wait to close the car door after he has gotten in. I know that they mean to be helpful, I try to discourage it. I say, "He can do it, can't you, darling?" They almost always get the message.

His daughters are especially prone to "doing" for him, which is natural enough. They are trying to help him but it isn't really helping him, he must keep using whatever skills he has left.

CHAPTER TWENTY TWO

DIARY June 6, 2003

We are back in New York. These have been very busy days. One doesn't just "move back", there is so much to do. I think I'm finally digging out from under. I've started my writing class again, which is the best medicine I could find. I really come alive there.

Linda has gone on her vacation. I hope he takes to the new caregiver. She came this morning and though she surely isn't Linda, she is very sweet. She talks a blue streak, which makes me crazy, so whenever she is here I try to duck out. Norm accepted her quickly, perhaps because she was here a day with Linda so she wasn't sprung on him. However the last two days he hasn't wanted to move and has complained of severe dizziness. When I got home yesterday at about one-thirty in the afternoon he was asleep on the couch in the family room and she, her name is Sonya, was sitting there and watching him. She said he had even been too tired to smoke (!) so she just let him sleep. He slept peacefully until about six-thirty and then woke and asked where we were going for dinner. We met our grandchildren, Sam and, Erica and had a lovely dinner. I won't pretend that he was the life of the party but he was there.

Today he again said he was too dizzy to get up. We were really worried so I took him to the doctor this afternoon. He had an EKG, a blood test, his blood pressure taken...absolutely perfect, 135 over 85 and his lungs, ears, nose and throat checked. Everything was normal. I don't think he was faking, but what it was I can't imagine.

October 27, 2003

Music seems to have a great effect on Norm. One night last week we went down to the other end of Palm Beach and had dinner with our friends, Larry and Elly Heller and Grace Forrest, all people with whom he is very much at ease. Still, he never said a word the entire evening. Coming home in the car I put on a CD of old Bing Crosby songs. I tried to coax him to sing but he just wasn't inter-

ested. Then Crosby started to sing the Whiffenpoof Song…a Yale favorite. At that, Norman, the old Yale man, began to sing, with expression and gestures. He knew every word. I almost started to cry. As long as the song lasted he was clear and totally "with it". When it was over he lapsed into silence again.

Then yesterday at a performance of someone imitating Maurice Chevalier he again sat in stony silence until the actor started to sing "Mimi" at which time he began to sing along with him, a big smile on his face. He may be a mono-tone but he sounded like Pavarotti to me.

I don't seem to lose the capacity to be surprised by a sudden flash of memory or by a further loss. I never know what he is going to take in and what will just confuse him further. One evening in an effort to keep him up until nine o'clock, I put on a video of the life of Eleanor Roosevelt. He watched transfixed and when it was over he said, "I always loved Eleanor Roosevelt. I remember when she came to see us on Guadalcanal." He seemed to have grasped every detail of what had been an hour's program. He would have watched it all over again. So I try to find videos that I think will interest him. World War II, and anything connected to airplanes, especially in the Pacific theater, will always keep him awake. Then there's football, both the games on Sunday afternoon and the ones on Monday night.

Norm has become almost Pavlovian in his conditioning. When he comes in the front door he says, "Can I go to bed now?" I am always looking for reasons to keep him up, at least until nine o'clock. A televised tennis match sometimes does the trick. Of course he will say that he doesn't want to watch but then he will give in reluctantly and soon he will be fixated on it. It also helps if I put out a coke and something to nibble on.

I find it fascinating that once he has become interested, his whole demeanor changes. His eyes lose that vacant look and he speaks in his old deep voice, rather than the babyish voice he now uses. About an hour or two is all he can take but that's really all I had hope for. I am more and more convinced that keeping his mind and body active slows down the progress of the disease.

One day I felt so low that I sat down at my computer and wrote the following.

LETTING GO

Can a brain feel flaccid? If it can, mine does. If that's not the right word, how about desiccated or worn out or just plain empty? And not just my brain but my body and my spirit as well. Sometimes I feel as if all my strength has been sucked out of me.

Yesterday I started to drive home from an afternoon with friends when I felt as if my car was behaving very peculiarly. It was jerking back and forth and it seemed as if the whole frame was going to fall apart. I was driving my Lexus and thought of the dealer's boast that nothing ever goes wrong with a Lexus. I couldn't imagine what it could be. Perhaps I should pull over to the side of the road and call the AAA, I thought. I vetoed that idea and decided it must be a tire beginning to go flat. I was only three blocks from home, the tire didn't feel completely flat and I was sure I could make it. Somehow I'm always sure I can make it. I often do, but I also seem to buy a lot of new tires. There must be a lesson in that.

As I drove into the driveway I noticed a small red light blinking at me from the dashboard. What it was telling me, and had apparently been trying to tell me since I started the engine, was that my emergency brake was on.

Is there a parallel there to how I feel now? It may be a stretch but it makes sense to me. I have been living with a constant brake on my emotions. I can't let myself go. I can't lose my patience. I have stopped being a free agent. I may try to move ahead, to remain calm and loving, but sometimes it isn't easy.

Yet for every day that I feel everything is too much for me, there is something to buoy me up. I remember one night when Norm woke me up saying, "I'm really trying"

"Trying what?" I asked.

"Trying to remember, but it isn't easy. I do have Alzheimer's, don't I?"

"No, darling," I said, "You have a bad memory like most of us at this age. Now go back to sleep."

He smiled as if greatly relieved and closed his eyes. Maybe this doesn't sound like a good thing to most people but to me it showed a greater awareness than I had given him credit for.

CHAPTER TWENTY THREE

Every time we go to Dr. Sadowsky he does what he calls a 'mini-mental'. It goes like this…"Norm, what is the name of the city you are in? Who is president? What day is it today?" (Since every day is almost the same as every other here in South Florida I think it's an unfair question). This sort of query is followed by "Please take this paper, fold it and hand it back to me with your left hand." Then Norm is given three words, common words like tree, book and glass. He is told to remember them and that he will be asked about them later. Then he is given a piece of paper and told to write a sentence. He usually writes, "I love my wife." Then the doctor asks him to repeat the three words. Sometimes he can and sometimes he can't, but then the same is true of me.

One day, about two years ago, the doctor finished the tests and said, "This is good news." He explained that the first time Norm took the tests, about six years ago, he scored 27 out of a possible 30. The next year it dropped to 21 and the year after that to 18. Since then it has remained at 18 but, the doctor said, "Today its back up to 21." I couldn't see any change, certainly not for the better, but if the expert thought it was good news I knew I should be happy about it.

One always has to be on the lookout for new discoveries. In 2002 I read in an Alzheimer's publication that there was a new drug called Mementine which showed great promise. Our doctor had certainly heard of it but told me that for the time being it was only available in Germany. He wished me luck in getting it and said that he would be glad to monitor it if I could get it. I mentioned it to a very dear friend of mine and he told me that he had a cousin who was a psycho-pharmacologist in Berlin. Next day he called me and said his cousin would be glad to help. His cousin was wonderful. We had the medication within a few days. In a week Norm was on his first dose and in three weeks he was at the full dosage. I was busy keeping my fingers crossed but not letting my hopes get too high. Has it done any good? That's a question I ask myself constantly. One answer is that I have no idea of how he would be without it, but considering how long he has been ill we must be doing something right. The truth is that I am willing to try anything considered safe that seems to hold out the hope of progress.

The drug is now readily available and widely used in the United States under the name of Namenda. Norm still takes it, but I can't judge if it is helpful or not. The progress of his illness has been very slow, so maybe it is working.

March 26, 2004

This morning Norm and I had a kind of birthday party charade. Last week I was showing Linda some placemats I had bought. She said to me, "You always buy yourself whatever you need. What does that leave for me to get for you from Mr. Winik?" I said that I would hide these and before my birthday she could take them back to the store and have them wrapped in birthday paper so he could give them to me. Friday morning she did and they have been sitting waiting to be unwrapped. Since then I've made a production of asking, "Should I open my present now or wait until my birthday?" He'd look at me with a puzzled expression and say, "Wait". This morning, with Norm sitting there, I finally did open it, to the sounds of "Ooh, just what I needed." Does it matter? I'm not sure, but I like to keep up the pretense of normalcy, it certainly can't hurt. I know that seeing me happy makes him feel good.

Most of us who are caregivers have to listen to a lot of well meaning advice. I wrote this after a good friend suggested that I put Norm in a nursing home.

Gratuitous Advice

One day our good friend Joe called. He was one who had stuck with us. He said that he wanted to ask me something important. I'm sure that he meant it kindly. He's a kind man and couldn't have known how his question would throw me.

Norman and I had had lunch with him and his wife on the previous Saturday. Joe really loves Norm and always tries to engage him in conversation. He usually manages to do it but Norm has gone deeper into himself lately and this time he didn't respond. He is more confused these days and rather than show his confusion he just opts out. He certainly did nothing strange at lunch but his silence was thunderous.

"Elaine," Joe said, "You may think I have no right to say this but I must. You are great with Norm, but don't you think it's too hard on you? After all, you have to live your own life."

How often had I been told that? He paused for breath and then began to say exactly what I didn't want to hear.

"Have you ever thought of putting Norm in a..."

"Joe," I said, "I know what your question is and the answer is no. First of all, I'm lucky enough to be able to afford to have a wonderful woman who stays with him five days a week, so I do have some free time. Fortunately he can dress, bathe and feed himself; all he needs is a little prodding. Can you imagine how he would feel if he woke up during the night and didn't see me next to him?" I should have added how sad I would feel if I didn't see him next to me.

All morning I've tried to shake my feelings of sorrow and anger. Not anger at Joe, I know he meant well, but anger at the values of the world we live in. Aldous Huxley, in his book, "Brave New World" said that the philosophy of that world would be "Ending is better than mending." Value only that which is shiny and new. When something is broken, throw it away and buy another. It isn't a bad idea when applied to inanimate things. We've all had the experience of finding that it's often cheaper and easier to buy a new toaster oven or electric coffee maker than to get an old one repaired. But it can not and must not be applied to people. Who said, "Hate the sin, love the sinner"? I hate Norm's illness and what it's doing to him...and to me. But I love him and so I settle for those times when he emerges from the fog in which he now lives.

I wonder if anyone thinks the situation through before they ask such a question. Dump my husband who still tells me twenty times a day that I'm wonderful and that he loves me? Then I could "live my own life." What a ball I'd have! Wherever my body was my head and heart would be with Norman.

Surprise all you kind friends, I am living my own life. I wouldn't know how to live anyone else's. That my life at this point is not what I would like it to be, I admit, but it's the life I have and my only option is to do the best I can with what I've got.

CHAPTER TWENTY FOUR

Since this is supposed to be my story as well as Norm's I will write about the wonderful thing that has happened to me. Between Norm's illness and my back problems, which have been pretty severe, I have been somewhat depressed. I have begun to feel old and tired. Now I have started to teach a class in creative writing. I just parrot those things I've learned from Louise Albert, my long-time writing teacher, but the results are amazing. The women write beautifully and say they love doing it. So do I. While I am teaching, and for a while afterward, my old verve and sense of adventure returns. I feel rejuvenated and better able to handle whatever comes up. It's so good to do something creative again.

Coping With Tragedy

One terrible result of failing memory is that each time a tragedy is remembered it hurts as much as the first time. Norm's younger daughter, Bette, died of ovarian cancer at the age of fifty-five. While she was sick, for about a year, we didn't tell him. We did go up to Boston to see her after she finished her chemotherapy. She wore a scarf on her head so as not to frighten him. To her credit she tried to sound well whenever she spoke to him on the phone. With me she could let her guard down, but she always tried to protect him. I certainly would have made up some excuse and gone to Boston for the funeral, but when she died I had the flu and couldn't even go out of bed.

I didn't tell him when she died. I felt that if he didn't ask I shouldn't volunteer information that would hurt him. Then one evening we were coming down in the elevator on our way out to dinner, when he turned to me and asked, "Did Bette die?"

Once he had asked, I wasn't going to lie to him. I said, yes, that she had died. He said nothing. About three days later he woke me in the middle of the night and asked, "Did you say Bette died?" I said that I had.

"What did she die of?" he asked.

"Cancer," I said.

"You see," he said, "That proves it's genetic. Her mother died of cancer too."

Then he started to cry, telling me, "You don't know how awful it is to lose a child." After that he would wake me almost every night to ask if Bette had died. Each time I would tell him that she had, the pain would be as bad as if this were the first time he had heard the news. I try to comfort him by reminding him of how much she loved him and how happy she was when we came to see her a few months before she died. That seems to ease his pain a little and he usually says, "It really made her happy to see me?" I assure him that it did, he goes back to sleep and then the whole thing is repeated the next night or the night after. He has a picture of Bette next to his bed. The other night, after he had awakened in tears, I asked him if he would like me to move the photo because it seemed to make him sad. "No" he said, "It does make me sad but I want it here."

He has as tendency to have bad dreams and many of them are about Bette's death. Then he wakes me up to ask again if Bette died. When he isn't dreaming of her, he sometimes wakes me shouting, "He can't do that!" I ask him who can't do what. Sometimes it is someone in the Marine Corps, sometimes a person he hasn't seen in years and other times all I get is a sheepish grin and, "I don't know, darling." I assure him it was only a dream and he goes right back to sleep. Sometimes I do too.

Routine

Routine is terribly important when dealing with a dementia patient. There is security in knowing that day after day he can count on doing the things he has become used to. Norm has gotten used to having a cigarette after breakfast. Of course he would have it before breakfast if we would let him. Truth to tell, if the phone is ringing or I haven't finished making breakfast, I sometimes give in. But the usual routine goes something like this:

Norman, "Can I have a cigarette now?"

Me," Finish your breakfast, darling."

Norm, "Then I can have one?"

Me, "Of course."

Repeat the foregoing about seven times and you get the picture of the mornings at our house. Sometimes I could throw the whole breakfast into the sink......but somehow I never do.

The minute this charade is over and he has smoked his cigarette, I go with him into the bathroom and hand him his pills. He looks at them and asks "Do you want me to eat these?" (I've given up telling him it's take these, not eat these.)

"Of course, darling." I say with a smile. "There is your glass."

Then I hand him the soap and tell him to wash his hands. Next comes the tooth brush. "What do you want me to do with this?" he often asks. Sometimes I ask him what he thinks he should do with it and he says, "Brush my teeth, of course." He knows but he has so little self-confidence that he has to ask the same question over and over. Finally he gets into his bathing suit and we are ready to go for a swim.

Before we get to the door, he always asks, "Can I have a cigarette now?" I tell him that he can have one when we get to the pool, hoping that he will forget by then. He usually does. However in the middle of our water aerobics he often turns to me and asks for a cigarette. I put my hand in the top of my bathing suit as if taking out a cigarette and ask him if he'd like a wet one. He smiles and I'm never sure of whether the question is a remnant of his sense of humor or just a reflex.

When he has spent the day with Linda, he walks into the apartment, takes one look at me, says he is exhausted and asks if he can go to bed. Linda tells me that when I'm not around he doesn't act quite that way. He has a little more pep and is more likely to ask for something to eat before he takes a nap. He seems to have developed certain habit patterns, reacting to me in one way and to her in another. I guess I'm a softer touch, although she is always so sweet with him and he loves her.

Weather

I have found that Norm is very sensitive to changes in the weather. That shouldn't be a great surprise to anyone since we all are to some degree. I know that I am. Still it always seems to come as a shock to me when after a day of his being very vague and out of it that I realize the humidity is about ninety percent. Another result of nasty weather is that my patience is affected. I have severe sinus trouble and it's hard to be calm and patient when your head is aching. I try to schedule relaxing activities for rainy days. He still enjoys movies and concerts and never sleeps through either of them. Although he never remembers what he has seen or heard. Still it helps to pass the time.

Loss of Confidence

As soon as you decide that you know ever nuance of this confusing disease, something will happen that takes you by surprise. Tonight as I was getting Norm to bed I handed him his toothbrush with the toothpaste on it. He turned to me and asked, "What do you want me to do with this?" Then, without waiting, he put it into his mouth and started to brush his teeth. "What do you want me to do with this?" has become one of his mantras, as well as, "Can I have a cigarette?" He will also come home at about four in the afternoon, get undressed, sit on the bed and ask if he can go to bed. I don't really think it's a lack of awareness as to what he is supposed to do but rather a lack of confidence in his ability to assess the situation and respond correctly. As I have said before, loss of self-confidence is one of the most tragic aspects of dementia. Before all this happened I used to tease Norm and say that he invented mental health, he was so secure and untroubled.

Sleep Patterns

Norman's ability to sleep for hours and hours never ceases to amaze me. Of course his sleep is usually restless, punctuated by cries and moans. I know how frightening his dreams must be since I am awakened almost every night with something like, "Hurry and let's get out. The house is on fire!" I am always able to rouse him and tell him that it's just a bad dream. He takes that in, smiles and goes back to sleep.

Somehow this second sleep seems more restful than the first.

Touch

A few months ago Norm exhibited a new symptom. If we were sitting in a restaurant eating dinner and someone came up behind him and tapped him on the back he would jump and in a terrified voice ask, "What the hell is he doing?" Obviously he was frightened, but then so was the well-meaning person who had only wanted to be friendly. Thank heavens it doesn't happen too often, but last night it did and his reaction was almost violent. I grabbed his hand and told him that it was all right. Then I reassured the gentle woman who, trying to be friendly, had evoked this response. As soon as things settled down I turned to him and said that he must never do that again and that no one was out to hurt him. I asked him if he understood and he said yes. On the way home in the car I tried to reinforce the message.

Will it happen again? I'm sure it will. The sad thing is that to me it's a sign that he lives in a frighteningly precarious world where any strange touch is a threat to his safety. On the other hand he has a constant need to reach out and touch me, to make sure that I am nearby. When we are outside in the sun, sitting in deckchairs side by side, a table between us, I am usually reading or writing something. He is constantly reaching over to take my hand. Since this makes any concentration on my part impossible, I sometimes try to pretend that I don't see his hand. He will have none of that, He'll just bang on the chair to get my attention. Then he holds my hand for second, smiles broadly and goes back to wherever he was before.

At night when I am in the kitchen getting dinner ready he calls in to ask what I'm doing. The truth is he really knows what I'm doing. What he wants is to make sure that I'm there. When I sit next to him on the couch or lie next to him in bed he keeps reaching over. He touches me just for a second, reassures himself that I am there, and goes back to sleep. I love when he does it, even if he wakes me out of a sound sleep.

I said that Norm's reaction to being touched when he doesn't expect it would manifest itself again, and the other day it did. We had gone over to visit a friend. When I stopped the car the doorman reached over to help Norm. Norm didn't see him coming *and* reacted very violently. "What is he doing to me?" he shouted, pushing the frightened man away.

"He is just trying to help you," I said, "and you can't talk to people that way."

His whole demeanor changed. He got out of the car, turned to the doorman and said, "I'm not sure what I did to you but if I hurt your feelings I'm sorry." I couldn't believe it.

People often tell me how much more alert Norman seems, living with him every day it's almost impossible for me to see that. There are moments, yes, but being with him almost constantly I am never sure if it is a momentary aberration or a sign that a medication is working.

A Good Surprise

Just when I think I'm about to give way to despair, something happens to lift my spirits. Yesterday we took Norm for some neuro-psychiatric tests. Besides the questions; what day is it? What state are we in? Who is the president? There are the instructions; fold this piece of paper in quarters, write a sentence, and count backward from one hundred by sevens. (Something I pray no one will ever ask me to do) Then blood must be drawn, urine collected and height and weight taken. A normal person would be a little upset by all of this, so you can imagine how poor Norman reacted. He was so jumpy and so anxious.

When it was all over I drove to a cute little restaurant we go to very often. Once we got there Norm didn't want to get out of the car. He kept asking if we couldn't go home now. Finally he did get out. We ate and then went home where he fell into bed and went right to sleep.

I woke him a few hours later, he dressed and we went out to dinner with very close friends. At dinner he was his usual silent self. Still, he didn't seem unhappy. He liked the people we were with and didn't seem too withdrawn. He said good-night quite cheerfully. We dropped the others off and then we were in the car alone. I had put on a CD of songs of our vintage. Usually he listens and once in a while he even chimes in. Not last night…last night he sang every word of every song. He sang in a loud clear voice and even mimicked the singer's voice. He was really enjoying himself, totally conscious of what he was doing. As for me, I was in a state of pure joy. Here was my old Norman, if only for the short ride home. One learns to take joy wherever one finds it.

Fear of Flying

Any change in routine is a problem for a dementia patient and coming back up north after spending the winter in Florida was certainly a change for Norm We got on the plane and he seemed a little jumpy. As an ex-pilot he always second guesses the pilot's maneuvers. I sometimes remind him that in World War II when he flew, the planes had propellers' and if you wanted to find your altitude you stuck your head out of the cockpit.

"Perhaps flying a jet is a little different." I suggest.

He smiles, and as soon as we are safely off the ground he usually goes to sleep and sleeps for at least an hour, or until food is served. This time he stayed awake for the whole trip and even watched part of a movie. He didn't even seem worried when there was a little turbulence. Of course the minute we got home he fell into bed and slept for hours. I only wish I could have done the same.

What We Still Have

I do get a lot of pity, unasked for and unwanted, from well-meaning friends. "Poor Elaine," they say. "What a hard life you have." I am not Stella Dallas, the heroine of an old movie who relished the sacrifices she had to make for the person she loved. I try not to dwell on the things we have lost. On the other hand, while I don't pretend that we haven't lost much, I just try to concentrate on what we still have. Not because I'm some kind of noble soul but because that is my way of coping. I have said that each of us in this situation must cope in his or her own way. This is my way.

I try not to think of the trips we can't take and concentrate on things like the following: Norm can be sitting outside on the deck when I hear him call for me. "Winquie," he says his nickname for me." Please come here." I go out with a pretty good idea of what will happen next. I am right. "Winquie," he says, "I need a kiss." How many women of my age get that request ten times a day? Of course ten times a day may be a bit much, but repetition is name of the game with dementia. Repetition and still more repetition.

Hope.

Optimist that I am I have a constant struggle with the concept of hope. The old adage says that it springs eternal and with me it does. The greatest problem with it these days is that it is usually followed by disappointment, but with this illness, one never says never. Here is a case in point. When we eat at home we watch quiz shows like "Wheel of Fortune" and "Jeopardy." I think that brain teasers are good for Norm. He used to be able to answer most of the questions on these shows, but in the last few years, he just sits and watches. Every few minutes he'll ask me, "What's this all about?" The other evening he answered a question correctly. An aberration, I thought. Then he answered another one and then another. Could the medication be working? I thought for the thousandth time. And then my admonition to myself, "Don't get your hopes up." (Norm does not do a lot of talking so I have conversations with myself. Not a bad thing as I almost always get the answers I want.)

The next morning I tempted fate. "Do you remember you answered so many questions last night on Jeopardy last night?" He broke out in an impish grin and said, "Of course I do." The usual answer is a sheepish, no. There goes hope again. What the hell I tell myself. Enjoy it for as long as it lasts.

Manners

A person with dementia will sometimes forget some of the social niceties. At dinner Norm will put his fork or spoon, from which he has already eaten, into the serving dish. I try to remind him gently to use the serving spoon. He does it once, and then goes back to using his own. He also has a tendency to belch loudly at the table. I've almost given up trying to stop that.

He is so fixated on his own feelings that he has lost the ability to empathize with others. I have been made aware of this the few times I have felt sick. I tell Norman that I don't feel well and that he'll have to look after me for a while. He smiles and tells me he'll take care of me. Two minutes later he asks me for a Coke or a cookie. If I try to explain that I don't feel well and that he should get it for himself, he will look a little sulky and tell me that he doesn't really want whatever it was he had asked for. I guess inertia is stronger than greed.

Fear of Dying

One of my great fears is that I will die before Norm. He is so dependent on me that he would be lost if I weren't there. I know that his daughter would put him in an institution, and I can't blame her, but I also know that he couldn't survive that. We used to say that we would die at age ninety something a little drunk, going over Niagara Falls in a barrel. Now we couldn't fit in a barrel…even if we could maneuver ourselves into one. I comfort myself by thinking that there's no point in worrying about things I can't control. Maybe that's not the greatest comfort in the world, but I have to prioritize my worries and that's not near the top of the list.

Doing Too Many Things At Once

Last night I invited a dear friend for dinner. She is someone Norm likes very much and is very comfortable with. I don't really like cooking, but I knew this would only be a matter of grilling steaks, mushrooms and peppers on an outdoor grill. I've done it hundreds of times and I know it's not a difficult thing to do. Or at least it never was before. What I hadn't counted on was that, the thermometer having reached ninety, every time I went out to check on the meal in progress, the heat would hit me. Besides that, every time I opened the door, Norm would get very nervous. "Where are you going, Winquie?" he would ask. "Are you coming back?"

To which question I sometimes answer, with a smile, "No, Darling. I'm never coming back." Then we both smile. He knows it's a joke. But he is obviously nervous at my going in and out, so he does what he always does when he's nervous, he eats.

When I came in with our guest's better done steak he had almost finished his and two bottles of Diet Coke. "Darling," he said in a very needy voice." I need another Coke. NOW" Emphasis on NOW.

I almost lost it. "Wait a minute, darling," "I said, with a slight edge in my voice "I haven't even had time to take a bite of my dinner and you're almost finished." He got the message and looked like a child who had been told to go to bed in the middle of his favorite television show. Not his fault, I told myself. He is living in his own world and I must remember that. I can't be involved in anything time consuming when we are together. I can't be a cook, a hostess and a caregiver all at one time. One might think I would know that by now but I keep learning new things and relearning old ones. Another day, another lesson.

Aches and Pains

Norman and I have reached that age when arthritis is almost a given. Sore knees and thumbs are part of normal life for those of us on Social Security. I know it and while I may complain and even groan a little, I take a pill and go about my business. It's much harder for someone with dementia. Norman knows that something is wrong. He hurts but doesn't know quite how to express it. His usual reaction is to wince a little, especially when walking. Then he asks to go to bed, not because he is tired, but because sleep is a refuge from all those things he can feel but can't explain.

CHAPTER TWENTY FIVE

RUSHING
ELAINE K. WINIK

The hours move so slowly
I count the minutes, pushing time away
As if the next hour will bring something new
All the while knowing it won't
And still I am impatient when the light turns red
When the line at the grocery store moves slowly
Have I really got something to do?
Or do I rush just to get back to nowhere
For nowhere is where my life is now

    I reread this poem and resent my having said that my life is nowhere. I still have plenty to live for, and Norm is part of that plenty.

DIARY May 19, 2004

As you can see from the poem above, I'm at fairly low ebb at the moment. Norm has really gone down, especially in his affect. *He wears that zombie-like expression and all he wants to do is sleep…for a change. Last night, coming home from the concert, or should I say the first half of the concert? I lost it. Maybe I was overtired, maybe I was worried about when Linda goes on her annual vacation and maybe it is my usual reaction to every big step backward. Whichever it is, I am feeling down. By the way, in my next life I intend to see all the second acts I've missed.*

CHAPTER TWENTY SIX

I feel as if our trip is getting bumpy. Worse than that, whenever I hit a new rough spot in the road I feel shaken and unsure. What's the matter? Will I make it? Where is my sense of humor, my old assurance? Can they really be gone? They can't be. I must try harder.

I used to dream of new worlds to conquer, of exciting adventure trips Norm and I would take. Now I dream of lying on the beach somewhere on the Indian Ocean, (it's my dream so I can pick my own ocean.) The sea is the requisite clear blue, the breeze warm and gentle. You get the picture; you've seen it in innumerable ads for tropical resorts. Best of all there is no pressure, no phone, no one who needs my attention. What about Norm? I can't allow myself the luxury of dreaming about the old Norm. That would make the return to reality too painful, so I just pretend that he's inside our small casita and will join me in a few minutes. Yes that's where he is, I tell myself. All is well. I can lie there under the palm trees a little while longer. I can lie there a little while longer but I can't live in my dream. I must live in the real world where I just have to keep going. How? I have to remember that I need some time for myself, time to release my inner brake and move more freely in my own world. The question remains, will I allow myself to do it? I can't promise. I can only try.

Incontinence

Unfortunately incontinence is a problem most of us will face. Whether it's from the dementia or simply age, I don't know. But I do know that as time goes on Norm has more and more trouble staying dry. At night we do give him what I have said we call sleeping pants, and by day we have started to put a small pad in his underwear. The one thing we never do is tell him that his underwear is wet. All we do is help him take the wet clothes off and throw them in the washing machine. Our machine may work overtime but Norm, who has always been meticulous, is spared embarrassment. He would be mortified if he knew. Maybe he does, but we try to make light of it. Instead I tell him, "Darling, at our age we all leak a little. These pads save laundry." No embarrassment, no anger. If he could help it, you know the story, he would be dry.

Rainy Day Problems

I have spoken about what I call "rainy day problems", those days when it's nasty outside and we have no special plans to meet friends. Norm is more than content to spend the whole day in bed while I try to dream up activities, even when said activities are nothing more than going to the pharmacy to pick up a prescription. "Go without me, darling," Norm will say. How can I explain to a grown man that I won't leave him alone in the house, but that I'll go crazy if I don't get out? My usual reaction is to say, "Sleep half an hour more and then we can both go to the store." It seems to work.

I must also come to terms that spending a day in bed won't alter the course of Norm's illness. But it still makes me nervous when all he wants to do is sleep.

Keeping Him Active

This morning we went for a swim. After about twenty minutes in the water Norm began asking if he could put on his bathrobe. "In the water?" I asked with a smile, "It would get soaked." He smiled back, but a few seconds later he repeated the question. This time I told him that we would swim another ten minutes and then he could get out. That didn't seem to be the answer he wanted. He looked at me and did something very unusual for him. "I told you I wanted to get out now," he said in a very strong voice. I realized that I couldn't get into a battle of wills with him so I just changed the subject completely.

"I have to call your cousin Franny," I said and we were off on a family discussion. He started to ask me about this or that one of his cousins, for a while that kept, us busy talking and swimming. I can't say that it lasted for a long time, but it did keep him in the water, and active, for another little while.

Dreams

Norm's dreams never cease to amaze me. One night he woke me calling out, "I raise." I've never played poker but from somewhere I pulled out the response, "I'll see you," I said. With a note of triumph in his voice he said, "I have four queens." Without any hesitation, I answered," I have four kings." He said "Damn" and went back to sleep. This morning he remembered nothing of the whole incident but he named each of the men who used to play in his poker game, which was fifty years ago.

"Didn't you say you were going to buy me a crossword puzzle book?" He asked at about 3 A.M. "I'm bored and I'd like to do a puzzle." Of course I had bought him a crossword puzzle book, but he had refused to look at it. "You've got one, darling," I said, "We'll do it tomorrow." "Good," he said and turned over.

Another night he started screaming, "What are you doing to me?" The look of panic on his face terrified me. I shook him gently and told him he was having a bad dream. "Who is that guy standing over me?" he asked. "Open your eyes, darling," I said, "There's no one there. It's only a bad dream."

He looked, smiled and went back to sleep. I wonder if these dreams are a side effect of one of the drugs he takes. There is no way to tell except by taking him off the medications, one by one, and that I'm not willing to do. We seem to have kept him at a relatively good level and it would be too much to risk to change things.

Sometimes I wake up a little shaky and then the following happens: Norm is the other room with Linda. He calls out to me in a cheery voice, "Winquie". I answer, "Hi darling", and then as an afterthought, I say, "Is Linda taking good care of you?" The answer comes back like a shot, "Of course, doesn't she always?" And my spirits lift. I'm off on my rollercoaster, happy again.

I have a friend who calls me a Pollyanna and perhaps I am. But as I said at the start of this book, each of us must find his or her own method of coping with a situation we never dreamed we would have to face. My way is to seize every small moment of hope, even knowing that it can't last long.

DIARY September 28, *2004*

This afternoon I took Norm to Dr. Sadowsky, the neurologist who has been seeing him for about seven years. Last week Norm had taken the usual tests and today we were to get the results. Apparently...and amazingly...he has not changed at all, at least not on the tests. Of course I see changes, but normal aging could be responsible for that.

The doctor said he was doing a drug trial with a new medication that acts on the amyloidal deposits on the brain. He said it was very promising and that he would like Norm to try it. It is a test that allows the patient to remain on his or her present drugs, like Remynyl and Namenda, and to add one more. This one is called Alzamed. He added that while in most cases half the patients get the real thing as opposed to a placebo, in this test two-thirds get the drug. It certainly seems worth the effort. He doesn't promise miracles but feels certain that it will slow deterioration. At age eighty three who can ask for more?

He also told me that the way I interact with Norm is wonderful and that he wished I could advise other caregivers. I wish I could too. I would really like to get this diary in some sort of order so that I could get it published and be of help to others in this position.

DIARY October 5, 2004

Today Norm started the trials for a new medication. We have no idea if he's getting the placebo or the real thing and won't know for almost a year. My fingers are permanently crossed.

Diary September 4, 2005

It is now September 4 and Norm is still in the trial. I still have no idea of whether he is on the full dose or on the placebo. We did go down to Florida for a few days in August so that Norm could be checked by the doctor. Of course we got no results, and from what the nurse told me even they don't know which patient got which dosage. He did as well on the mini-mentals as he had done before. One funny thing happened, a new nurse gave him one of the tests and said to me, "He's a mathematical genius." I could have told her that without all the testing.

CHAPTER TWENTY SEVEN

I have devoted the better part of a lifetime to the up building of Israel and to helping to rescue the remnants of the Jewish people, and I have loved every exhilarating moment of it. Yet today I have to force myself to read about the bad news from the Middle East. I don't want to hear of tragedies about a place and people I love. So I turn off the television, put away the paper and do a crossword puzzle. As I stay home and watch Norm disintegrate little by little, I tell myself that I have to save my strength and my empathy for him. I have to be there to help bridge the ever-widening gap between his perceptions and reality. When he looks terrified I want to hug him and assure him that I'm there. That seems to be the only thing that gives him comfort and if it takes all my energy...so be it.

Yet I can't sink into bathos or self-pity. There are those with greater troubles than I have. I at least have support systems to give me some room to breathe, and though I sometimes have to persuade myself of this, the world does not revolve around me. So I have come up with a set of rules for myself and anyone else who might want them...no charge

Rule 1: Get out and away for a little time everyday.

Speak to other people., Even the slightest interchange can bring some discovery. One day I went to the post office to mail a copy of a book I have written to a new friend. "Book rate please' "I said to the woman who was weighing the package and then added, "I wrote a book and now I'm spending a fortune mailing it to people."

She laughed and said, "I'm retiring next year so I can write a book too."

"What about? I asked.

"How my Italian immigrant parents came to this country and coped with life here." She added, "I also have a novel in my head. The idea came to me about three years ago, just out of the blue." She went on at length describing the plot which sounded interesting but did not please the people in the now-long line behind me.

It was a nothing incident and yet I left the post office feeling much better than I had when I came in. Not only had I distanced myself from my self-absorption but I had spoken to someone involved with something creative, someone who was looking forward.

Rule 2: Do something physical.

Amazing what a mood elevator a swim can be. Of course it ruins the hair, but what the hell, you can't have everything.

Rule 3: Don't lose your sense of humor

Maybe that should be rule one, two and three. Look for something to laugh at. Laughter can pull you out of the slough of despondence before it gets too comfortable in there. I don't mean jokes, although they can sometimes help, I mean seeing the humorous side of a situation. Sometimes that's a stretch, I agree, but I keep trying. Can you imagine seeing the funny side of locking yourself out of your car in the pouring rain and then losing the key as I did last week? Doesn't sound funny, does it? But it's better to laugh at one's foibles than to cry. In the scheme of things it's only a glitch and not a tragedy

Rule 4: Don't get into tests of strength.

If he wants to do something you really don't want him to do…i.e. go to sleep at 7:00 pm. instead of arguing, change the subject. People with dementia are easily diverted. Remind him that there is a great football game on and that you want to have a Coke and sit in front of the TV and watch. He will probably think it's a good idea.

Rule 5: This is a very important one

Don't look in the mirror any more than is absolutely necessary and NEVER look in the magnifying mirror. This rule is one I rarely abide by as I sit at my dressing table and notice a long hair on my chin and an age spot on my forehead. Norm often walks in to find me at this and I say," I need a porter for the bags under my eyes."

He looks at me, smiles and says, "You have no bags darling. You're beautiful". So I smile as his answer, true or not, has cheered me up. Then I mentally add an addendum to Rule 5 "Stay behind your face. What you don't see won't hurt you. I decide that if I smile, others may be shocked at the change in my looks but at least I'll be able to put it out of my mind. That is, until the next time I have to look in the mirror.

Some wise soul said, "Laugh and the world laughs with you…" you know the rest. You also know that it couldn't be more accurate. After all, others have their own troubles and aren't the least bit interested in hearing about yours. Who can blame them? We don't want to hear theirs either.

That's all for now. How much sage advice can I dish out at on time?

On rereading the excerpts from my diary I can see that while most things are worse, some are a little better. Norman no longer wakes up shaking and telling me that he is too sick to go out. He has given up asking for Hoss Moss and other long-gone Marine Corps buddies. His walking is much worse, especially up and down stairs. Linda and I are always at hand to make sure he doesn't fall, and he now carries a cane. When we go to the pool in Florida we have a walker on wheels. I love it because it helps him and it also gives me a place to put lunch which we eat outside at the pool. We also have a wheelchair, which Linda uses when she takes him to the park or to the mall. When she asks him to get into the wheelchair he is so grateful to be sitting that he doesn't feel any embarrassment being pushed around.

At this point in our lives I have given up keeping a diary. The days pass, one good day and one not so good, but there is a sameness to them. I try to keep him stimulated…and myself as well. There are times when I want to cry but I wouldn't change places with anyone. Do I wish Norm was well? Of course I do, but he isn't. In spite of that there is enough of Norm left to keep me going.

This morning Linda and I were talking and I said to her, "You know, I have really had a fairy tale life." I thought a minute and then added, "But fairy tales always have happy endings." She looked at me and said, "This is a happy ending." She was right. What tomorrow will bring I don't know, but today we we're together and at our age that's sort of a minor miracle.

The other day in my creative writing class we were assigned the topic of three wishes. I want to share what I wrote.

What would I do if I were granted three wishes? When I was a young girl I knew the answer to that, "All sick people should feel better. All poor people should get money and everyone should be happy.". To be honest what small child would think that way? Those wishes must have been imposed on me by my highly moral and caring parents. All honor to them, but I wonder how they would have responded in the privacy of their bedroom.

I'm sure that both my mother and father would have wished that he could regain his health. That doesn't seem selfish to me, it seems normal. What would I wish at this point in my life? I would wish to wake up one morning and find Norm up and dressed. He would say to me, "Get up lazybones. Let's go the bird sanctuary. It's time for the bird migration and we might see all kinds of warblers." I would get up, drink the orange juice he had just squeezed, get dressed and we would spend the next two hours wandering through the bird sanctuary. He would nudge me and say things like, "It's a Virginia Warbler" I, with my Audubon book at hand would say, "I'm not sure. It might be an Olive backed Warbler." We would discuss that weighty matter for a while as we looked at the pictures of all the one hundred or so warblers, as if identifying this one bird was a matter of great importance.

When we got home he would say, "Let's plan a trip. We haven't been away in months. Where would you like to go darling?"

I would tell him that I have always wanted to go to Dubrovnik. Then, warming to the subject I would add, "We could see the remnants of the old Jewish community and then drive all around the countryside. Our kids Margot and Kenny did just that last year and loved it. They said they slept at small inns or bed and breakfasts the whole time and never stayed at a hotel" I knew he would like that kind of informal trip and truth to tell, so would I. We could rent a car in….. Enough…I'm getting too caught up in wish number one. You do understand that the foregoing is only one wish, a long one it's true, but no one said they had to be short wishes.

I still have two more wishes. I'm not sure I even want them. Oh, health and happiness for my children and grandchildren, a nice husband for my daughter Penny and one for our granddaughter Jill, the usual things one wishes. The old Hebrew wish is to live to one hundred and twenty. I called my niece's mother-in-law on her one hundredth birthday and wished her that. Her answer came quickly, "Please," she said, "Don't wish that on me."

She was right, I don't wish for long life…I've already had that, but I do want to live just one day longer than Norm. He would be so completely lost without me.

So what has happened to poor people, and to sick ones? What about world peace and a little peace and quiet in Israel? What about a change in government here in the United States? Three wishes just won't do it. It would take at least one hundred wishes, and then I would still have left someone out. I think I'd prefer just slogging along and trying to do the best I can without the help of some fairy godmother.

Giving me three wishes is like putting a starving man at a table full of food and telling him to eat his fill. He won't get healthy on the meal, he'll probably stuff himself and then throw up. So don't tempt me with these wishes. They won't come true and I'll be left with nothing more than emotional indigestion.

This morning I went to Doctor Sadowsky to discuss some treatments that had been suggested to me by a neighbor. He said that the medication in question was untested and certainly unproved. He then told me that Alzheimer's is such a complicated disease that progress on a cure has been very slow.

"But Norm doesn't have Alzheimer's, does he?" I asked. "Somehow it has always been comforting to me that what he has is called a dementia. Anyway," I added, "he doesn't get angry the way Alzheimer's patients do."

He looked at me with a sad smile and said, "Elaine, call it whatever you like but only about 25 percent of Alzheimer's patients are violent. I would certainly classify him as suffering from an Alzheimer dementia."

As I sit here I wonder what difference it makes what label is put on his illness. It is what it is and we both will live with it…I hope for a long time.

I want to end this book in the way that I started. Dementia is certainly not what anyone wants, and yet a good part of the time, life can be pleasant and even fulfilling. The moments of clarity, the smiles, the times I hear, "Darling, I love you. You are so good to me," bring comfort and joy. When I get into bed at night and he reaches over and pats my arm I am content. Whatever the future may hold…and I don't kid myself on that score. I am so grateful that he is still with me. Our life together has its share of pain, but it has its share of joy as well. There are rewards to be found even in this kind of situation.

Perhaps the greatest reward is the knowledge that you have not failed the person you love.

ABOUT THE AUTHOR

Elaine Kappel Winik, the third of four daughters, grew up in New York City, where she attended the Fieldston School. Her father, an immigrant from Russia became a very successful businessman, taught his children to live by his ethical values. Her mother, by shining example, taught her and her sisters that steady kindness and humor can get a person through many difficult situations. After attending Connecticut College, she married, raised three children.

Her first love was Democratic politics, but having seen at first hand the remnants of the Holocaust she volunteered with the United Jewish Appeal. Rising in the ranks she became chairman of the Greater New York Woman's Division of the UJA and finally national chair and then national president.

Her "job" as president of the National United Jewish Appeal took her around the world. She got to know Eleanor Roosevelt, Helen Keller, Golda Meir, David Ben Gurion as well as Yitzak and Leah Rabin. She is the recipient of the Israel Education Fund's Ben-Gurion Leadership Award, the Harriet Jonas Award from the American Jewish Committee and the Louise Waterman Wise award from the American Jewish Congress. For her work in bringing a high school to the town of Dimona in Israel she was named the First Honorary Citizen.

At fifty, and divorced, she met Norman Winik, a widower who developed sports clubs and camps. They fell in love and married. Together they traveled the world and lived a seemingly charmed life. Eleven years ago, Norman Winik began to suffer from dementia. What the high-powered Elaine Winik brought to his care and their relationship will be heartbreaking and eye opening for those readers who are faced with the responsibility for a loved one. Winik's first book *Still Looking Forward* was praised for its lively account of her life and work before her husband's illness. *Living With Dementia* deals with a darker chapter in her charmed life, but Winik never loses her sense of humor—or her kindness.

978-0-595-38373-3
0-595-38373-4

Printed in Great Britain
by Amazon.co.uk, Ltd.,
Marston Gate.